Deckhouse

My Story

Donat Le Blanc

authorHOUSE®

AuthorHouse™
1663 Liberty Drive
Bloomington, IN 47403
www.authorhouse.com
Phone: 1 (800) 839-8640

Published by AuthorHouse 05/28/2020

ISBN: 978-1-7283-6306-6 (sc)
ISBN: 978-1-7283-6307-3 (hc)
ISBN: 978-1-7283-6305-9 (e)

Library of Congress Control Number: 2020909772

Print information available on the last page.

Preface

My story begins in 1972, while I was attending Southeastern Massachusetts University. One of my classes was the course "Death and Dying." We were asked to write a short story on a personal experience relevant to the title of that class. I received a grade of B-plus, with a comment by the professor that my story should be published in a magazine. I shared my story with another arm amputee, a female civilian friend struggling a similar amputation. She commented I should publish my story in *Argosy* magazine. As time went on, this short story got bigger and bigger. My career and marriage made it difficult to write, but I would eventually write down the events that I remembered. Years passed, and classified information from the Vietnam War became declassified after twelve years, in 1988, so I was able to download my squadron's Command Chronology Reports for the period of April through October 1966, the time I was there. This was eye-opening for me, confirming things I remembered but had put to the back of my mind so as not to deal with things I had experienced.

It wasn't until my father passed, and then my mother, that I started to research my father's military background and his life experience. This is when I discovered his POW experience and could gather the documents he was holding onto that he had never shared with me. It happened when my mother asked me if I wanted the information; otherwise, she was going to throw it away. So much information—my grandfather's green card, the discovery of my grandmother's gravesite, etc.

My retirement from the government gave me the opportunity to gather this information and at the same time as I could deal with my own combat experiences. This time gave me the courage to ask for help at the PTSD clinic for much-needed counseling. I had theorized that by throwing myself into my work, I never dealt with my PTSD, at least not professionally. I did not do so until retirement, when I began to feel useless and had great guilt for surviving. I was also dealing with the death of so many friends after the war that I made the decision to ask for help.

Many thanks to my Marine Corps squadron members, who I meet with infrequently, as well as my local Vietnam veteran friends, for their friendship and comradery.

Of course, I need to thank my wife, who has put up with me for the last thirty-nine years. I love you so much for everything you do for me every day. Many people don't realize what assistance you provide for me, as well as our children and grandchildren, who keep us all going. She knows how difficult life has been as an amputee, and more recently, since I've had numerous surgeries on my remaining limb. It has been discouraging at times, and if not for you, my love, I know not where I'd be. This story is for my family, but if others have interest it the events of my life, and if it helps you, then it has been worth the time.

Chapter 1

My Early Years

My story begins with my earliest memory of my father. He was very tough on me, to say the least, even in the very early years of my life. As a young boy, no more than five years old, I can remember very well the treatment I received from him.

Wedding picture of my parents

I was born April 10, 1946, in the whaling city of New Bedford, Massachusetts—or more precisely, in the town of Acushnet, at the former

Acushnet Hospital. My parents had been married nine months earlier, on July 4, 1945, while my father was still on active duty in the United States Army during World War II. He was married in his uniform.

Four months after their wedding, on November 16, my father was honorably discharged. He had been drafted November 9, 1942, and served three years. He was involved in the D-Day invasion on June 6, 1944. Two months later, on August 2, my grandfather, who is my namesake, received a Western Union telegram. It was sent to him by the US War Department to notify the family that my father, George E. Le Blanc, was reported as Missing in Action (MIA) in France.

War Department telegram

Between August 2 and 15, the family received at least twenty-six postcards and letters from all over the United States and Canada with the same message: it had been reported over shortwave radio that Private George E. Le Blanc, service number 31227310, born on September 20, 1921, had been captured and was being held as a prisoner of war by the German Army; he was safe and well in France.

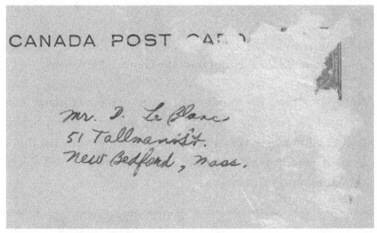

Two postcards from Canada and the US

On August 15 the family received another Western Union telegram from the War Department informing them that my father had been the subject of a shortwave radio report. Unofficially, he was now a prisoner of war, pending confirmation. In today's world, this lag in information may seem incredible—now families receive almost immediate notification and confirmation when a soldier is wounded, captured, or killed in action.

Kriegsgefangenenpost

Postkarte

An

Gebührenfrei

Absender:
Vor- und Zuname:

Empfangsort:

Gefangenennummer:

Straße:

Lager-Bezeichnung:

11875
U.S. CENSOR

Land:

Deutschland (Allemagne)

Kriegsgefangenenlager

Datum:

Kriegsgefangenenpost

Postkarte

An

Gebührenfrei

Absender:
Vor- und Zuname:

Empfangsort:

Gefangenennummer:

Straße:

Lager-Bezeichnung:

U.S. CENSOR

Land:

Deutschland (Allemagne)

Kriegsgefangenenlager

Datum:

Two white V-cards sent from the German POW camp

After his capture, my father's first correspondence home was sent on December 26—the day after Christmas and some four months after his capture. There were two other postcards or V-cards (as they were called), both sent from him while he was held at the Stalag 7-A prison camp in Moosburg, Germany.

Part of camp Stalag VII A at Moosberg.

Stalag 7-A, Moosburg, Germany

On April 19, 1945, my grandfather, PePeré Donat J. Le Blanc, died of congestive heart failure at the age of fifty-three. Just eleven days later, on April 29, my father was liberated from Stalag 7-A. He was sent to Camp Ramp in France, an American facility, on May 9, and finally returned home in June, one year after the D-Day invasion. He had been held as a prisoner of war for ten months.

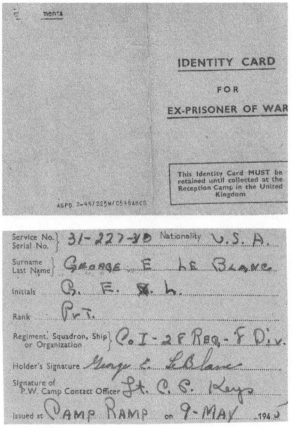

POW Identification card for Camp Ramp

Dad spoke very little of his years of military and wartime service or of his capture, at least not to me. I often wonder what effect the death of his dad, of which he never spoke, had on him. I wish he would have been a little more open and forthcoming with me, his only son, about his military service and his experiences—it may have helped me to understand him better than I did as a child or growing up as a young man, or as an adult or later as a disabled combat veteran myself. You would think we had a lot in common, but we didn't, or so it seemed to me—except that we both suffered from post-traumatic stress disorder (PTSD) from our combat experiences. He was service-connected 50 percent for this disorder, and I am now 100 percent, with a number of disabilities, the worst of which is the amputation of my right arm.

Most of what I have learned that I recounted above was discovered only after my dad had passed away. I learned about him from my mother and from his only sister, my aunt Doris, who passed away still sharp as a tack at the age of ninety-two in 2017. I have also learned that my father lost his mother, my grandmother, when she was twenty-six years old and my father was only two. He never spoke to me about his mother's death, and I knew nothing of her until recently, thanks in part to Aunt Doris and Ancestry.com. I discovered that upon her death in 1923, my grandmother was buried in New Bedford in an unmarked grave. So I've taken it upon myself, with my aunt's permission as my grandmother's only living child, to have her grave marked. Maybe it's my own sense of life and death now that I have turned seventy-three; those things have greater significance and meaning to me now.

Chapter 2

Life with Mom and Dad

My mother passed away on Mother's Day, May 8, 2016. Mom and I got closer the last several years before her death. Dad had died at the age of seventy-one in 1993. In my opinion, Dad lost the will to live, becoming very depressed as he was extremely dependent on Mom. He wouldn't get out of bed, so as a result, he was hospitalized at the local Veterans Administration Hospital in Providence, Rhode Island. He was placed on oxygen, and for a few months, he was catheterized and fed by a nasal gastric tube. Then he was transferred to a nursing home near our home in New Bedford, where he died after only one week.

After his death, Mom moved from Florida, where they had been living with my oldest sister and her husband, to live closer to me and my mother's family of brothers and sisters. Mom was very independent until about six years before her death, when she had numerous falls. She received a diagnosis of multiple myeloma bone cancer, and after three years of weekly chemo injections, she had finally had enough. There was yet another very bad fall and a fractured leg and ankle, followed by a bleeding ulcer and more falls. All this occurred while she was living in an assisted living facility. I could see that she was failing.

At the end, her heart was very strong, but she had not taken any food or water for nine days. Finally, at 6 AM that Sunday morning, on Mother's Day, I got the call. My wife and I rushed to her bedside to see her take her last breath, and she went peacefully. Her death hit me very hard, harder than I thought it would. Having seen death and dying far too often in my life, I thought that I had developed a kind of carelessness or acceptance of the inevitable, and I always felt that I got my strong exterior and resilience from her. But I still today miss her and my dad both very much, and I miss those conversations we didn't have.

During the early years of my childhood, my father was my personal hero, even though our relationship was very difficult because of his treatment of me and what seemed to me to be his emotional distance. During his army life, he served as a military policeman with the Seventh Military Police Battalion out of Camp Edwards, Massachusetts. He served in northern France and participated in the D-Day invasion in 1944. He served with Company I, Twentieth-Eighth Regiment, Eighth Division, and was discharged from the 704th Military Police Battalion at Camp Edwards as a private.

I was the first child born to my parents and the first male grandchild in the family. I was the favorite of my mother's parents, PePeré and Memeré (Grandpa and Grandma) Gaudette, and all the aunts and uncles, at least for a short time. With eighteen other cousins and siblings born over the next eighteen years, my favored status was somewhat short-lived. But still we were a very close family because of my grandparents, and that memory of those early years will stay with me fondly forever.

As I have said, my father was very tough on me even when I was a young child. He was very stern and distant and a hard man to figure out when it came to his son. He was, I thought, harder on me than on my two younger sisters. I remember at the age of five being tied by a long rope around my waist to a tree in the backyard of our home so I wouldn't play in the driveway or go into the street. My mother would attest to this story and admitted to my determination. I would spend hours untying the knots so I could get away and go to my grandfather's grocery store, which was next to our house. There, he would offer me candy and soda. What a great memory: the smell of that store, which I can recall even now; my PePeré wearing his white smock and Stetson hat, his cigar in his mouth, cutting meat and bagging groceries. I have his Stetson to this day.

Life was very difficult for my parents. We had little money, and both Mom and Dad worked very hard. Dad had a sixth-grade education. But we were a close and happy family. When Dad would get home from work, he would get very angry with me because the candy and soda would spoil my dinner, and also because I had left my toys in the driveway—a big mistake for me. I was only five years old, but I still have memories of the eighteen-inch ruler he used to take to my backside. Corporal punishment was the rule of the house, at least when it came to me.

These are good but in some ways difficult memories of a young man growing up, but today, I credit his sternness with my ability to deal with the hardships dealt to me all many years later, when I was in my twenties and thirties. I think that my dad's experience in the POW camp and the loss of his parents wasn't wasted on me. His way of getting me to hurry up as a young boy was to yell *"Roush!"* This was German for "hurry up." *"Roush! Roush!"* he would yell, and I sometimes didn't move as fast as he thought I should. I paid the price for not being fast enough for him.

Chapter 3

California Living

When I turned six years old, in 1952, my family decided to move from New Bedford, Massachusetts, to Long Beach, California, like everyone else in the 1950s, for a better life, thinking that the streets were paved with gold and lined with orange trees. The part about orange trees was true—at least for a while. Dad and Mom took advantage of the VA's GI Bill Home Loan program and bought their first home. They paid about $10,000 for a three-bedroom home in a new housing development where they had to cut down orange trees to build houses. What a shame. It was a wonderful place to live and grow up. I so enjoyed those years of my youth from first grade through my sophomore year in high school. What great memories.

All those kids I knew growing up are now lost to me, only to be remembered in my own mind. They've moved on, as have I. Most have passed on. Others have moved to places I do not know. I will remember those years forever, especially my years playing baseball and football and my first job as a paperboy. The first newspaper I delivered was the *Long Beach Independent—Press Telegram*, an afternoon newspaper. Back in those days, we would ride our bikes to a designated house located somewhere in the neighborhood to pick up our newspapers for our assigned routes. The papers were picked up from a paper mother, who owned the home and who counted out our papers according to the route manager's assigned number of deliveries for each carrier that day. On average, each carrier, about twenty kids in total, would deliver about thirty-five to forty newspapers each day. We would sit around in the driveway of the paper mother's home and fold the newspapers—depending on the thickness of the paper, either in half for thick papers or in thirds for thinner papers. We folded according to the number of pages reported on the front page of the newspaper. The daily paper was between fifty and one hundred pages thick. This was a daily ritual six days a week.

On Sundays, we would ride our bikes to a different location further away from my home to a local grocery store. Usually the Safeway supermarket, and pick up our Sunday newspapers from the delivery truck driver for an early-morning delivery, usually at 6:00 a.m. This was so we wouldn't wake up the folks in the neighborhood. The daily papers were usually smaller than the Sunday, which meant for me, two bike rides to the supermarket or one slow ride with all the papers back to my home. Back in those days, we were charged for the newspaper bags that we carried the papers in, as well as the rubber bands we used to secure the folded newspapers. The Sunday paper was usually delivered flat because of its size.

The company paid us by us collecting a monthly fee from each of our approximately fifty customers. The bill was sent to our homes each month. We were issued a metal collection book with cards for each customer indicating how much to collect each month. Some customers received newspaper-related material other than the newspaper, which we collected for each month. The customer's card had a tear-away ticket (receipt) that was pulled and given to the customer when they paid the carrier. Every month, the newspaper would mail the bill for our monthly newspapers, plus magazines, directly to the customer that we had to collect for. We got nothing for it but were responsible for collecting the fee.

Back then, the average cost for a newspaper was $2 per month, delivered to your home. If our bill was $65 for forty customers, after we collected the $65 and mailed a check to the newspaper, the balance remaining was our pay. That meant for forty customers, we earned about $15 for the month, after expenses. We earned practically nothing for three hours a day on average, seven days a week—that's twenty-one hours for less than $15 a month, or 50 cents a day (16 cents an hour). Even then, I felt as if I was working for nothing, but I did it for about four years. Tips were minimal, and you wouldn't believe the people who couldn't come up with the $2 every month. Christmas tips were okay but not great. Even back then, I remember having to chase customers for the lousy $2 that belonged to me. Ice cream from the Good Humor man was a dime. That was a treat.

Then I heard about another newspaper, the *Los Angeles Times*. A route came open. It was not as close to my home as the *Press Telegram* but was still within a bike ride from my home. It was mostly apartment buildings, and they would deliver the papers right to my house for delivery. All I had to do was deliver the paper, and they would collect the fee and send me a check at the end of each month. That sounded like a great deal to me, and for a fixed fee of $30 a month. *Now we're talking*, I thought. The only problem was the Sunday paper was 300 to 400 pages thick. The daily was around 100 to 150 pages. When I saw my first Sunday paper, I cried. How many trips would this take me? I had saddlebags and a box on the handlebars of my bike, so I could carry about thirty to forty papers on Sunday at a time, and I had about eighty papers to deliver. That meant two trips on Sunday. At fourteen years old, I was whipped by the end of my deliveries. The other issue was that it was a morning newspaper, which meant getting up every morning before school at 5:00 a.m. At least it kept me in great shape.

As time went by, I talked my mother into helping me on Sundays. I was able to deliver the dailies, but the Sunday paper was enormous. Back then, we had a 1956 blue Ford station wagon. I called it the "Blue Goose." I would load the back of the wagon at five in the morning with my papers on Sunday, I'd wake up my mom, and she would put on her robe, still in her pajamas, and drive me on my route. I would never think of waking my father, because I knew he would be angry at me. (I tried once.) Mom, on the other hand, was more willing to help, especially if I cried. I would sit on the tailgate of the station wagon and run to the houses and the apartments, dropping the papers on the doormats. That first Christmas, I remember getting $49 in tips alone from people whom I'd never seen or met. All thanks to my mother, who knew I was having a very hard time helping with even the daily papers.

I remember telling my Uncle Leo back in Massachusetts about the size of the *LA Times* Sunday paper. He didn't believe me, so he ordered a subscription. When he got his first Sunday paper, he called and told me, "Hell, it takes me all week to read the Sunday paper." That was because it was mostly classified ads. I was always angry at my father and disappointed in him for not helping me with the Sunday papers. I don't know why except he worked six days a week at his job in the grocery store. He worked as the assistant manager, while Mom worked five days a week at the Bank of America as a bookkeeper. I truly appreciated my mother for her help back then. I know it was hard on her, but she knew it was also very hard on me as well.

We had moved to California with one of my mother's sisters (Claire) and her husband (Maurice). I looked up to both of them as my other mom and dad. Both have passed away. We lived in California together, although in different cities, until 1962, when my aunt, who was very home sick and decided along with her husband to sell their home and move back to Massachusetts with their two daughters. For me and my two sisters, moving sounded great. What an adventure! We had no concept of the difficulties my parents would face. What would they do for work? Where would we live? We needed to buy winter clothing and other supplies. But the pressure was on my dad, with seven against one in favor of moving. It was more than he could handle. Regardless, my parents decided to sell our home and move back East to Massachusetts at the same time as my aunt and uncle.

I left to go back East with my uncle earlier than the others that year. I drove across country with him in his Buick station wagon, just the two of us. He was great, and we had a great time driving across country together. His wife and two children flew home, and my father and mother, along with my two sisters, drove across country after our house was sold. I wish I had stayed because my father threw away my *MAD* magazine collection and all my baseball cards. What would they be worth today? He did this, he said, to save room in the moving van. Damn, that pissed me off then, and it still does to this day.

Chapter 4

Who Am I?

Through my years at school in California, I always went by the name "Danny," thinking that this was my real name. I remember in the ninth grade a teacher telling me my name was Daniel not Danny. I argued with her that it was. All my school records read "Danny J. Le Blanc."

Then, when we moved back to Massachusetts, my mother took me to register at New Bedford High School for classes in the eleventh grade as a junior in high school. New Bedford requested my transcripts from my high school in California, Milliken High School, and the information that was returned stated that they had no record of me, so my mother and I went to New Bedford High School to find out what the problem was. It was only then that I discovered at the age of seventeen, my mother had given the Massachusetts school my birth certificate with my real name of "Donat," not "Danny."

All through school and even in the military, I was teased with nicknames like Donut, Jelly Donut, and so on. I had forgotten some of them until, when attending a United States Marine Corps reunion in 1996, some of the guys I had served with in Vietnam referred to me as DJ. My wife thought that was odd because my youngest son, Donat J. Le Blanc Junior, has always gone by the nickname of DJ. He too has accepted his name without question, and to this day, he goes by DJ.

I remember even in my early years in California, at the age of ten, playing Little League baseball. A neighbor took me under his wing, seeing something special in my abilities. I had good skills, and I was a tough kid, so I played the position of catcher on the Little League team. I did some pitching as well. I played extremely well in my youth.

I was upset that my dad never came to one game all through my years of Little League, even through my junior high school and high school years and during my summer years playing in the CYO (Catholic Youth Organization) in Massachusetts, where I played baseball, basketball, and football. Never once did he make an effort to see his only son play ball. I know that work was a priority for him, but he couldn't even make it when I played on weekends, or later, as an adult, when my men's softball games were took place in the evening under the lights. He was not a jock and had no interest in sports of any kind. It killed me that he had no interest whatsoever in me.

In fairness to him, between the years 1963 and most of 1964, when we moved back East, Dad could not find work in the New Bedford area, having only a six-grade education and no marketable skills. His only work experience was in the grocery store business. It was very hard for him to find gainful employment with four other mouths to feed. He was finally offered and took a job in Connecticut working as a security guard for the Pinkerton security company. His pay was so low that my mother, who was working now at the Acushnet Company golf ball division, would send him money to live. Dad eventually took the civil service examination, and with his disabled veteran status, he got a job working at the Otis Air Force Base on Cape Cod, where else but in the commissary (i.e., grocery store), a perfect fit for him. It provided good money and good federal benefits.

Back to my ball-playing days, years after my return from Vietnam, in the early 1970s, I was asked to play slow-pitch softball by some friends in a local barroom league. It sounded like fun. I thought my ability to play ball had pretty much ended after my right arm had been amputated, but to my surprise and the surprise of many others, I was able to play and play at a high level of competence over the next twenty years. I was twenty-four at the time.

I heard that men who worked with my father commented to him about my ability on the softball field and how they would go every evening to watch the men's softball game. The men's softball league was exciting to watch, as it was very competitive. One evening, when I was playing, I was shocked to see my father pull up in is car to see me play. Wow! I was amazed. Later in the game, around the third inning, he would get into his car and drive away. He never said a word to me about it after that. I was glad and disappointed at the same time – glad that he had gone out of his way to see me play but disappointed that he didn't stay to see the entire game, but that was my dad.

Maybe that's the why I tried not to miss even a practice of any of my three boys' or my daughter's sports, whether it was swimming, baseball, basketball, football, soccer, or whatever. Today, I even attend my grandchildren's sports, because I know what it meant to me to have someone there just to watch me! I hope they realize it.

During the next few decades I played men's slow-pitch softball aggressively, until the age of forty-seven, when my first major injury occurred. I remember playing in the Boston VA Medical Center slow-pitch softball league, for the Prosthetics team. We were mostly amputees playing against abled-bodied players, and we played well. However, one evening after work, playing at the Brockton VA Medical Center softball field, after swinging at a pitch and miss hitting, the pain in my left arm was so bad that I dropped the bat and didn't even attempt to run to first base. I returned to the bench in great pain, knowing I could no longer play. I remember picking up my glove and my shoes, getting into my car, and driving home with my spikes still on. I finally made it home, in great pain. The next few weeks were terrible. Then, following a series of cortisone shots, I felt better.

Chapter 5

United States Marine Corps

In 1964, after graduating high school, I had to make a choice—get a job at the local mill, go to college, enlist in the military, or wait to be drafted. So I took a job in the mill, at the Titleist Rubber Division, with the help of family. Back then, if you didn't know someone already working in the mill, it was hard to get a job there. I worked nights, 10:00 p.m. to 6:00 a.m., with mandatory overtime on Sundays in the press room. I couldn't afford to go to college, having no scholarship money and lousy grades, and my mom and dad had no money to send me, so here I was, with no encouragement to stay in school.

From the age of about fourteen, my dream was to be a United States Marine. Even in junior high school, when my school counselor asked me what course in high school I wanted to take, either college preparatory or business, I said, "I want to join the Marine Corps."

He said, "That's not one of your choices," so I took the business course.

As I said, I worked in the mills from June of 1964, after graduating high school, until November of 1964, when I enlisted in the United States Marine Corps. My enlistment began in November 1964 as part of what was called the "Delayed Entry Program," so I would not miss being home for the holidays in 1964. I remember making that decision after receiving a notice from my local Draft Board Number 4, in New Bedford, to report for my draft physical in October of 1964. It was during that ride home, on the bus from the Boston AFES (Armed Forces Enlistment Station) that I decided I was not going to let the government tell me where and what I was going to do. I wanted to make that decision on my own. My draft number ended up being 219.

On that bus ride home, I met a young man named Vinnie P (not his real name) who was in the same situation as me. We decided we would join the Marine Corps together. The next day, I sought out my Marine Corps recruiter in the Customs House in downtown New Bedford. Sergeants Robinson and Cooper were the two recruiters, and I thought they were great guys. I still have the deepest respect for both men. I met Vinnie P there, and we both enlisted for four years as infantrymen (0311) grunts, with no idea what we really wanted to do. Maybe we'd get into tanks. Vinnie P and I left together for Parris Island, South Carolina, on a cold morning in February of 1965.

USMC Enlistment Certificate

During this time Indochina, as it was known then, would soon become Vietnam. It was just getting hot and heavy. When I got home that day in 1964 after I had enlisted, I went over to my father, who was sitting in his recliner chair, watching television. I told him that I had enlisted in the Marine Corps. His response was, "You don't have the balls." He didn't believe me, so I walked away from him and went into the kitchen, where my mother was preparing dinner. I told her the same thing. Her response was, "You didn't?"

I said, "Yes, I did," and added that I wouldn't be leaving until February of the following year. I remember that she cried. That is my last memory of any conversation with my parents about the military. I remember the holidays of 1964. All my friends and relatives were very nice, all wishing me farewell and good luck.

When February came, Dad and Mom both took me to downtown New Bedford to catch the bus to the Boston Marine Corps recruiting station, where we joined about thirty other men from all over Massachusetts. We all took our oath to the United States of America and the United States Marine Corps. Then, while waiting for the next hammer to fall (the bus ride to Logan Airport), the recruiters in Boston came into the waiting room, where we were all sitting. They asked if any one of us was interested in volunteering for the air wing as part of the Aviation Guarantee Program. We would be guaranteed this assignment if we volunteered. They said they needed four recruits.

While sitting in the Boston recruiting station, I had struck up a conversation with a young man next to me by the name of Mike M (not his real name), from Worcester, Massachusetts. We seemed to click. The Boston recruiter further stated that to qualify for this Aviation Guarantee Program, you needed to have a four-year enlistment and have a high school diploma. If we met those criteria, we would be guaranteed a job in aviation. Mike M and I looked at each other. We both had the four-year enlistment already, and we were both high school grads. He, in fact, had a college degree as well, so we raised our hands together, along with about ten other guys. They took four guys. Mike M and I were two of the four.

All of us were all eventually hustled toward the bus that took us to Logan Airport. We then boarded a plane to beautiful Beaufort Naval Air Station, where we were then bussed to the Marine Corps Recruit Training Depot at Parris Island, South Carolina, fondly referred to as PI. We had no idea what we were in for. Let the fun begin!

We arrived very early in the morning, around 3:00 a.m. Most guys were sleeping on the bus and were very tired. A drill instructor got on the bus and immediately started yelling, "Get the fuck of my bus, you maggots. Go, go, go, ladies. You're not moving fast enough. Get the fuck off my bus now! Move, move, move."

My first thought was, *What the hell did I get myself into?*

"Get on the yellow footprints. Hurry up, hurry up, you turds," he yelled. I found a set of yellow footprints and stood there silently. I don't know what happened to Mike M. or Vinny P. we all got separated immediately.

19

I was dressed in my penny loafers, khaki slacks, and a short-sleeve maroon shirt, and this was February. I didn't want to bring a lot of clothes, and was told not to, but it was still freezing cold. There was even ice on the parade deck where we were standing, shivering. The next command we were given was to march (*yeah, right*) to a holding barracks, where they had us pick a rack (bunkbed), get into it, and get some rest.

On the racks was a mattress and a pillow—no sheets, no pillow covers, no blankets, and no heat in the building. God, was it cold. I got no rest, no sleep, just lay there silent and shivering. Three hours later, in comes another drill instructor. Same thing again, screaming at us, "Get up, get up, get outside, you fuckin' maggots. Get on the footprints. Move, move, move!" We got on those yellow footprints again, and then we were taken to breakfast in the mess hall.

There we were standing outside at 0500 (5:00 a.m.). It was dark in the early-morning hours and cold as hell. We were shivering as we waited for the recruits already in training to go through the chow line in the mess hall. Oh, my God! Is that what I'm in for? I could see the marine recruits going through the mess hall for breakfast, the DIs screaming and yelling at them. *Holy shit*, I thought. Finally, it was our turn to go through the mess line. This would be my first exposure to SOS (shit on a shingle), chipped beef on toast. Yuck! In the cold air, it looked awful. I still don't like it, I think because my first exposure to it was at the beginning of the chow line, with the cold air putting a crust on the top. It just didn't look very appetizing. After chow, we were taken over to supply to draw our uniforms and then our first buzz cut. After that, we were escorted to our barracks, where we would live for most of the next twelve weeks. During the years that followed, this often changed then length of training that is as the need for troops increased the time was shortened.

Mike M and I finally hooked up again in the barracks as we were lined up in front of our bunks, in alphabetical order so that one rack separated us (L-M). We were then told to get out of our civilian clothes and empty our pockets and to put everything on our bunks. I had forgotten that my recruiter, Staff Sergeant Robinson, had given me a piece of paper that had my twelve general orders on it, and he told me to study it as it would help me before I arrived at PI. Well, did I listen? No! I had no idea what they were, but I was soon to find out. I had brought the paper with me only to find that this would cause me to have even more pressure put on me during my twelve-week visit to PI.

We had four drill instructors, three DIs and one senior DI. They were all going through the barracks looking at our stuff on the racks. Sgt. Ricker was at my bunk. A slim handsome Marine in great physical condition, he had, I would later find out, taught hand to hand combat at PI. He laughed, which terrified the hell out of me, asking if I knew Sgt. Robinson. I replied, "Sir, yes, he is my recruiter, sir." I learned quickly how to respond to every question put to me. He told me that he and Sgt. Robinson had gone to boot camp some years before together on the "buddy system" and that he would be keeping a special eye on me. He would also keep Sgt. Robinson apprised of my progress.

"So you better not fuck up, maggot," he said.

God, was I in the shits now. Vinny P was also in my platoon but did not have this same paper with him. He never acknowledged knowing Sgt. Robinson either.

My next memory at boot camp was getting our vaccinations. I remember standing in a line in our skivvies (underwear), facing another row of recruits as a corpsman approached and stuck a needle in our arm to draw blood. Then another came by to take it out of our arm— an assembly line of sorts. Needles never bothered me, so this was no issue, but across from me, a guy turned as white as his skivvies, and he promptly did a face plant on the floor. No one moved, and he just lay there. Then when this was over, we were told to face left and right and proceeded to get more shots with some pneumatic guns in both shoulders. This was another assembly line as we marched out to get our utilities.

As the weeks went by, I learned quickly and tried very hard to remain as obscure as possible. I got into the third of four squads in the middle of the platoon in an attempt to hide, but as the weeks progressed, and as recruits started to falter, I found myself near the front of my squad. Then, at last, I was in front. I had been assigned by the DIs as the squad leader of my squad of nineteen recruits. Now I was responsible for nineteen other recruits. *Why me?* I thought. I just wanted to survive this and get out of here alive.

Then it happened. The guide on—the guy who leads the entire platoon of seventy-six recruits carrying the platoon colors—went down. This happened while we were at the Confidence Course, which is yet another set of obstacles set up for us to complete during our twelve weeks of training. While we were on the "Slide for Life," the guide on fell off the cable into the water below, and when he hit the water, he hurt his ankle, so he could no longer march. Our next obstacle was our two-mile run, which was around a dirt half-mile track in full gear with our weapons.

The drill instructors picked me to carry the colors and be the guide on. I accepted this with mixed emotions—pride and fear. First was the pride I felt after the DIs had picked me and given me the honor and responsibility to carry the platoon colors. Then I thought, *That means I have one more thing to carry damn two miles in the dust and dirt.* Add to this the competition factor. Our recruit battalion was in what was called a "series": three other platoons in the 300-series platoons, 312, 313, 314, and 315, all running at the same time, competing for the best time head to head. The two-mile run was timed, and all recruits had to finish—"leave no man behind," as it were—within the time required.

As we were the last platoon in the series (315), we got to eat the other platoons' dirt first. Not a good thing, so we had to pick up the pace. The course worked this way: run a half mile, walk a quarter, run a half, walk a quarter, and so on until the two miles were completed. We could pass the other platoons only when we were running in full formation. We ended up passing the other three platoons and finished first in the series. This despite the fact we had a very fat recruit in our platoon who we purposely put near the front. We knew he would bail on us, and we *all* had to finish together with all our gear, or the platoon would fail, which was not an option for us. This was obviously designed to develop teamwork, so we kicked his ass all the way around the course. Each guy next to him took a piece of his gear—his pack, rifle, and rifle belt—and made sure he finished the course. All this for one more streamer on the guide-on pole, but we did finish, and we finished in first place.

Chapter 6

The Rifle Range at PI

Our last month at Parris Island was spent at the rifle range. After all, every Marine is first a rifleman. Then he specializes in some profession. I was to be an air winger, not knowing what I would be doing as a job. Our first few weeks were spent learning the working end of the M14 rifle, what the PMI (primary marksman instructor) called "snapping in," that is, pretending to fire real rounds or bullets at a target that does not exist. That meant lying in the wet grass in the very early every morning with the infamous "sand fleas," and they really do exist, and they really bite. After a few weeks of this boring shit, we finally got to go to the firing range with live rounds. There, we would test what we had learned and so the instructors could see if we had been paying attention.

At the range, we were required to qualify by firing from three different distances—200, 300, and 500 yards—in four different firing positions, standing at 200 yards, sitting and kneeling at 300 yards, and the prone position at 500 yards. The day before "Qualification Day," we had what is called "Prequalification (or Pre-Qual) Day". This is where the rubber met the road. All those men who were not paying attention and faking their practice time would pay for the errors of their ways on this day. On Pre-Qual Day, we would for the first time use live ammunition and mark our own shots in our own shot record book, and at the end of our day, we would tally our score for a score of either marksman, sharpshooter, or expert. I still have my shot record book today and cherish the memories of those days.

If you didn't fire at least a marksman score, which was the lowest qualifying score, you would be treated worse than a piece of whale shit. I remember that on Pre-Qualification Day, I was at the 200-yard marker, and my friend Vinny P. from New Bedford and I were on the range together. He was right next to me, just in front. We were all sitting on ammo boxes before going to the standing position to fire then after giving us the order to stand when he started to stand up from his seated position with his finger on the trigger of his M14 and the safety off. While trying to stand, Vinny P. leaned toward me and squeezed the trigger, firing a round about a foot in front of where I was sitting. Fortunately for me, he missed my foot, and unfortunately for him, the primary marksman instructor (PMI) and one of our DIs were both standing right behind me when this occurred, and they saw everything.

Me and my drill instructor at the rifle range

He was immediately pulled off the firing line, and they both proceeded to chew and kick his ass. It scared the shit out of me—the shot, that is—as well as everyone else who witnessed the event. On Pre-Qual Day, I fired very well and felt good about the next day, believing I would at least qualify.

The next day was Qualification Day, a big day in a Marine recruit's life. The night before, unbeknownst to us, the four drill instructors and the PMI each had picked one recruit in our platoon who they thought would fire the highest score the next day at the range. They each bet a case of beer, to go to the winning drill instructor. And yes, I was picked by Sgt. Ricker, while Vinny P was picked by another DI. The day of qualification, I finished second highest in the entire platoon, with a score of 227 out of 300, firing Expert and the highest score of the five recruits that were picked that day.

The worst thing that happened that day was that one of our four squad leaders, who was also picked as one of the recruits to do well, was caught altering his score on Pre-Qual Day. He did not qualify on Qualification Day. The poor bastard was extremely humiliated by the instructors. The humiliation was unbelievable, and I felt very bad for him. Marching back to the barracks, he was forced to march in the rear, with his cover backward, his weapon upside down, shirt out of his trousers. He was to march backward, carrying a flag that identified him as a non-qual.

We all knew nothing of the DIs' wager until that night, when I was called into the drill instructors' office and informed of the bet. I was told that I would be allowed to make a telephone call home that evening. I didn't get any beer that night, but I was given permission to call home as the winner of the competition—as long as I didn't get caught doing it by the fire watches.

This proved to be quite the adventure, as we were on the first floor of a two-story brick building at the rifle range. While there, each platoon had a fire watch, or a guard in their squad bay. I had to sneak out of my rack after lights-out and crawl to the hallway and not get caught by our fire watch. I would go to a location with a telephone booth and try to make a telephone call without getting caught by the other fire watch. I got to the telephone booth and noticed that the door was closed, and there was no light on inside the booth. When I pushed the door, there was already a recruit inside making a call, and he had turned the light bulb off. So I had to hide behind the booth until he was done. When he finished, I got in and made my collect call to my girlfriend back home, asking her to let my parents know that I had called, that I did not get caught doing it, and that I was doing okay.

During our time at the rifle range, I remember an occasion early on where we found a frog in the squad bay. The DIs told us that was our good-luck charm, so we had two recruits assigned to care for the frog in a small matchbox. They had to carry the frog back and forth to the range with us then, one day, the frog died, so now we had to provide the animal with a decent burial. We all went outside and dug a hole, and we had six recruits as pallbearers. We had a recruit play "Taps" on his lips, and we all acted as mourners. What a bunch of crap.

Chapter 7

Boot Camp Graduation and ITR

Graduation Day from PI was a tremendous relief and a source of great pride for my family and for me. Seven marines from each platoon, or 10 percent, would be promoted from private (PVT) to private first class (PFC), and one would be awarded a free set of dress blues, the sharpest uniform in the military. Each candidate would be selected by the drill instructors. I was selected for PFC by my drill instructors, a very proud day for me. Our platoon passed final inspection and also took every award and competition at PI. We also won the drill competition. We marched for final inspection and were a good-looking and very proud platoon of Marines. That day would be the first time we were referred to as Marines, not maggots or turds or some other derogatory term.

My graduation picture

PLATOON 315
THIRD RECRUIT BATTALION   M.C.R.D. PARRIS ISLAND, S.C.
SGT. R.L. WELLS   SGT. E.A. RICKER   SGT. J.H. KING   CPL. G.E. LOUPIN
MAY 4th, 1965   PHOTO BY J.F. MAAG

Parris Island Platoon 315 graduation picture

I was surprised that day to see my parents and my older sister, along with my then-girlfriend—all of them there to see me graduate—they all seemed very proud of me, although our time together would be very brief, as we were heading out the next day to the Infantry Training Regiment (ITR) at Camp La Juene, in North Carolina, where we would spend the next four weeks on compass training, weapons training, hand grenades, rifle grenades, Browning Automatic Rifles (BARS), combat training, rappelling, taking a town, as well as a lot of marching with full gear and the infamous gas chamber. I spent the afternoon with my parents, sister, and girlfriend. The afternoon flew by, and then they were gone. I don't remember much of that afternoon except that it felt very uneasy being with civilians again after twelve weeks of strict military order, which I liked.

Upon arriving at Camp La Juene, my boot camp platoon was split up. All recruits were separated by rank. All the PFCs from all of our series were brought together to select new platoons. I was assigned to the "R" Company (Rough and Ready).

Fourth squad leader of platoon in "R" (Rough and Ready) Company

All the PFCswere brought together we were sixteen in all in the company, forming for platoons, each consisting of four squads. Each PFC was allowed to pick the thirteen men who would be in their squad for the next month. I was the last PFC to pick. I was not sure why, so I got the last thirteen men who were not picked. I then found that I was the squad leader of thirteen men of color. This was my first experience with bigotry. They *all* proved to be great Marines, and I would find later that they would take excellent care of me.

I learned later that because Mike M had scored so high on testing at PI and had a college degree, he qualified for OCS and would go on to Officer Candidate School to be trained to become an officer. I would never see him again. I have written to the address I had, but the letter was returned. I have visited the Vietnam Wall many times, but his name is not there.

Not all my boot camp platoon went to "R" Company. We were split up, and I lost track of Vinny P—until one of our Sunday-morning mess hall trips. Sundays were very special at ITR because we could get fried eggs or eggs cooked any way you wanted them rather than the usual powdered scrambled eggs that we would get every other day. On this

Sunday, I was with some of my guys from my squad. While walking through the mess hall, I came across Vinny P, sitting alone.

I told my guys I would see them back at the barracks after breakfast, as this guy was a friend of mine from my home town. I sat with Vinny P, and we talked and finished breakfast. It was great to finally see someone from home. We walked back to our separate companies. His was across the road from mine (he was in "S" Company). We said our goodbyes and wished each well. During these weekends, almost all my squad stayed close to the barracks. We were a lot alike. We'd clean our weapons, rest and relax, and read—no drinking or getting into trouble.

My bunk was located along with the other three squad leaders in our barracks. We all slept in the same area, and our racks were positioned to the left as you walked in the front door of the barracks, two bunks together. Mine was the first bottom bunk. Later that same day, after meeting with Vinny P, four guys from another company came into our barracks looking for trouble. As I lay on my rack reading, all I heard was "There he is," and saw one guy pointing at me. I got up from my bunk and asked what they wanted and what was wrong. They began to berate me for eating with Vinny P that morning. These guys were really pissed and were there to do me harm. As these guys were getting in my face, my squad gathered around behind these four guys. One of my guys was a very tall and intimidating black man.

"What the hell is going on?" he demanded.

They told us they were from Company S and that Vinny P had refused to go through the gas chamber. Upon refusing this, the instructor said that because he had refused, his entire platoon would go through the gas chamber twice—once for themselves and once for him. It was because of this that Vinny P was blackballed by his entire company. For the remaining weeks at ITR, no one would speak to him or have anything to do with him—and anyone who did would pay the price.

I couldn't blame theMarines for the blackball. I wouldn't want to go through the gas chamber twice for anyone, and as we had already been through the gas chamber, we knew of the experience and had all successfully completed that part of the training exercise. The Marines departed without issue, and I never saw Vinny P again after that for many years to come. Our next meeting would come years later and be very interesting after all this.

During my time at ITR, we had numerous inspections of our weapons and barracks. One such inspection stood out in my mind. During this time, I had started smoking cigarettes, as many men do in the military. Unfortunately, we often had the smoking lamp turned off because someone was caught screwing up or sleeping during our outdoor classroom sessions. Many men turned to other forms of tobacco, such as snuff or chewing tobacco. It was during this time that I experimented with chewing tobacco as well. I only tried this outdoors because of the requirement to spit. Some men though chewed indoors and used spit cans obtained from the mess hall. It was during one of our Sunday surprise barracks inspections that I learned of this indoor habit.

While the entire platoon stood in formation on the road in front of the barracks, we heard a godawful scream from our barracks, followed by a crash. It seems one of the Marines in the platoon had left his spit can out of his locker. You see, the men would lock their spit can in their locker during inspections, until this one day, when one of our commanders saw the can and said, "What the fuck is this?" With his kaki dress pants and shirt on, he decided to kick the can.

What a mess—black spit all over his uniform. He then preceded, all pissed off, to toss the racks and lockers within his reach. After this, he came outside, and we paid the price—drill, drill, drill. Needless to say, this didn't happen again.

My time at ITR finally ended in late June of 1965, with orders to report to NATTC (Naval Air Technical Training Center), Memphis, Tennessee, for helicopter school, this after a week's leave at home. My time at home was all a blur. I remember very little of my week at home (11). All I could think of is where I was headed.

First leave home after boot camp

Chapter 8

NATTC, Memphis, Tennessee

I reported to the Naval Air Technical Training Center (NATTC), Memphis, Tennessee, in July 1965, where we first took—what else?—more testing to determine what we were qualified to do in the air wing. We were given three choices of jobs we would "like" to do. It happened for me that my first choice was clerical, and none of my choices were to be a mechanic. So what did I qualify to be but a "mechanic"? I was sent first to reciprocating engine school and all the other courses affiliated with it for helicopters, which included a class in jet engines. The Marine Corps was still utilizing reciprocating engines and some jet-engine helicopters at that time.

These classes were not fun, but the alternative was worse. Those Marines who failed at helicopter school were transferred to be grunts (infantry), not what you wanted in those years if you wanted to survive your youth. This would ring for me years later, as a friend of mine who was supposed to join the Marine Corps with me but was a year behind me in high school stayed to finish his high school education. Then, after I got home in 1967 from Vietnam, Bobby Gonneville joined the Marines. I encouraged him to go aviation, which he did, but I told him, "You've got to study and graduate from aviation school, or they'll send you to the infantry." He did go aviation, but then, on November 9, 1967, Bobby was killed while serving as a Marine infantryman in Vietnam. Bobby had failed in school and was sent to the infantry. Now he's on the Vietnam Wall in Washington, D.C. (Panel 29E Line 58) a very sad day.

Over the years, his parents have now both passed away. At the end of his father's life, he was in a nursing home. I went to visit him just once. He was sitting in the solarium. When he saw me, he lit up.

"Danny, how are you? Nice to see you."

He stood up and told everyone in the room that I was a Vietnam War hero and a close friend of his son Bobby. I then told everyone, "No, I wasn't the hero but rather Bobby was, and I added that Bobby had been killed in Vietnam". That was my one and only visit to Mr. G. I couldn't bring myself to return. Bobby was my first close friend from home to die in Vietnam. I saw a lot of death and severe wounds in Vietnam, but Bobby's death hit me hard. I knew I had lost a brother. I think of him every day.

Classes for me were challenging in Memphis. Actually, the base was located in Millington, Tennessee, just outside Memphis. In Memphis, we had a combined classroom and hands-on helicopter work. I did poorly in class but was successful in the shop work. Then, one day, I was called to the commanding officer's office to discuss my low test scores and grades. They wanted to review my notes during this meeting. I was also given an oral exam, which I passed with a high score. It seemed I had trouble taking written tests. All my notes were accurate and neat.

Later, I was appointed class leader because of my rank (PFC) and eventually did well in helicopter school. Following our schooling in Millington, in of 1965, the twenty marines in the class were assigned orders. The jet-engine marines were assigned to Quantico, Virginia to HMX-1, the president's squadron. The reciprocating engine class was assigned orders that read, "FMF-Pacific." That meant Vietnam.

Reciprocating engine class (1965) graduation.
I am in row 2, fourth from the right.

Reciprocating mechanics sent to Vietnam. I am second row, center.

A two-week leave was in order, but before we would be sent to Vietnam, we were ordered to report to Camp Pendleton, California, for Escape and Evasion Training School. Again, my two weeks at home were all a big blur. I reported to Camp Pendleton a weekend early, as did a few other guys, so I remember renting an apartment at Oceanside Beach to relax and take in the sun with a few of the guys I knew from helicopter school.

Chapter 9

Escape and Evasion Training in California

Escape and Evasion was quite the experience. We had a lot of trooping and stomping, as well as survival swimming, which we did at Memphis also. During the training, we were instructed on how to survive in the field—what to eat, how to prepare it, and how to avoid being captured and survive in the jungle. The last three days were very unsettling. On our last day of training, we were assigned to fire teams (groups of four) and had to travel from one mountain range through a valley area to another mountain range, by compass. We were ordered not to be captured by the enemy. We were each given a canteen of water, an orange, a carrot, and a bag of rice. Most fire teams we saw were captured. We were not. We thought we were just the cat's ass as we survived without being caught. That next day, in the outdoor class, the instructor showed us how to kill and skin a rabbit, which he did in front of everyone.

That night, while sleeping in the dirt, some of the guys broke into the instructor's rabbit hooch and let them loose, trying to capture some for food. The next morning, we would pay for that act. While we were sitting in the outdoor classroom, we were set upon by what seemed to be dozens of Communist troops. While a lot of guys tried to run away, we were all eventually captured.

We were then lined up, tallest in front, shortest in the rear, four lines of about three hundred men. We were then told to lace our fingers around the chins of the men in front of us. I found myself again in the middle row. Toward the rear of the company, we were then marched in what they called the "Bataan death march," in company formation for what seemed like miles to a makeshift concentration camp. When we arrived at the compound, we were separated by rank—all NCOs and officers in one area and all other enlisted in another compound.

I remember during the march, one of our guys tried to escape when he thought the guards weren't looking. What he didn't know was that besides the guards, immediately around us, there were also guards watching us from a short distance. We were told later that he tried to hit one of the guards, who proceeded to strike him with a rifle butt, after which he was taken to sickbay and returned to our barracks. More on this story later.

The sole purpose of the prison camp was to see if we had learned the lessons from the previous days about how to act and survive in a prison-camp situation. This time was very stressful for most of us. I remember being taken from the compound and told to load a truck with barbed wire in the hot sun. After this, I was placed in a 55-gallon drum that was in the ground on top of another drum. I was placed in the drum, and a piece of plywood with a small hole in the center of it was placed on the top of the drum's hole, letting just enough light into the drum to annoy me. The drum was narrow enough so that I was unable to sit or stand to get comfortable. I'm not sure how long I was in the drum. I remember that it was sweltering.

The worst of this three-day ordeal was the last day, after we had made numerous attempts to escape and formed groups to get food, water, and work details, as well as establish a chain of command, as we were taught. On that day, the camp commander, who was a British Royal Marine Captain, James Galsworthy, had us all sit in the compound in front of him while he berated us for doing exactly what we were taught, stating that if he was the Communist camp commander, he would have had us all killed. If that was not bad enough, they marched out in front of all of us ten marines with paper bags over their heads to hide their identity. Following both physical and water torture (waterboarding), they all signed blank pieces of paper later admitting to atrocities against mankind. This must have embarrassed these men. One of these men was one of the ten men I had gone through helicopter school with; we all knew he was afraid of water and could not swim well. When they performed the water torture on him, he broke. I never saw him again after that day. He was a good marine.

That day, we were taken by trucks back to the barracks area to the mess hall and provided with a full turkey dinner with all the fixings. It was great considering the meals we had been served there before. Most of us ate food from the "garbage truck"—hamburgers and hot dogs and cold subs. When we returned to the barracks after chow, we discovered the guy who had tried to escape. He told us his story and had bought all the sandwiches from the garbage truck for us, not knowing we had already had a great turkey dinner. He was pissed.

This was one of our last days in CONUS (Continental United States). We had the next weekend off before being transported to El Toro (MCAS) Marine Corps Air Station and flown to Vietnam. That last weekend was the first weekend in April 1966, my twentieth birthday. I was fortunate because I still had friends living in Long Beach, California, and when we had weekends off, I would take the bus from Oceanside to Long Beach and visit old friends. Those memories are good ones. Most of them have passed away. I still communicate with a few of them on occasion.

On Sunday, April 17, 1966, before we left California, the *San Diego Union* newspaper published an article about the Escape and Evasion School, entitled "Jungle Survival Isn't Easy, but Learning How Is the Making of a Marine." It included a full picture of the waterboarding used by marines on marines. Other pictures included the prison compound and a picture of Captain Galsworthy. I still have that newspaper article, which describes everything I've described. I have received wriiten permission from the newspaper to use this article in my book for this I am truly grateful.

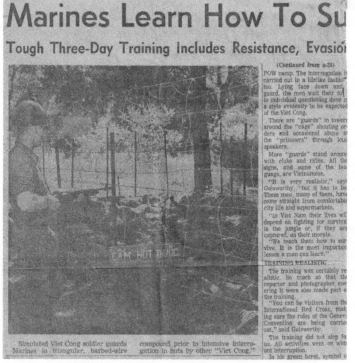

Newspaper article of the Escape and Evasion training

I personally experienced all this and will remember what we went through forever.

Chapter 10

Welcome to Vietnam

Two weeks after leaving California, we had a stopover in Okinawa for a week. Soon after that, I found myself in Vietnam, in late April 1966. On arrival, my most vivid memory is of the C-130 airplane door opening and encountering the heat and that awful smell. I was later to learn it was soy bean oil and fish oil, which was overwhelming in the 104-degree heat at the Chu Lai airfield.

Four of us—Darrel G, Richard B, Bob M, and I—were then transported by truck to the Ky-Ha helicopter airbase, just south of the airfield at Chu Lai. We had all graduated from Memphis helicopter mechanic school together and had been assigned to HMM-363 (Marine Medium Helicopter Squadron 363), a UH-34D Sykorski Sea Stallion Squadron. When we arrived, as was customary for new squadron Marine replacements, we were assigned some sort of work detail supposedly to allow us to get accustomed to our new temporary home and assimilate to the base and our new surroundings. Richard and I were assigned to mess duty. I was assigned to the "burn shack." This was a tent located near the base mess hall, where we had a number of responsibilities. The first was to prepare burners for the mess hall cooks to utilize in the mess hall for the preparation of each of the three daily meals. Each of the burners that we used had two tanks—one filled with gasoline, the other with compressed air. The gas tanks were manually filled with gasoline and the air tanks with a compressor. Unfortunately for us, the compressor we were provided was a gas-operated circa-1933 compressor, which was constantly breaking down. When that happened, we had to fill the air tanks by hand with a bicycle pump, not very much fun in the heat. We would bring the pressure up to 75 pounds in the air tanks, while the temperature in the tent was over 120 degrees. On average, we would fill ten to twenty burners for each meal.

Working in the burn shack required us to get up very early in the morning. Our first job was to light the submersion burners, of which there were twelve. These were used by the Marines to clean their mess kits—two rows of six, three with soapy water and three with fresh water for rinsing. Because it was early in the morning and because the submersion burners were located just over the hill from the officer's tents, we had great joy in lighting the burners by putting a little too much gasoline in the burner and throwing a lighted burn stick into the gasoline can. This would ignite the gas, creating an explosion. As we did this in rapid succession down the two rows of the six burners, it sounded like rockets going off early in the morning. The officers and cooks would get really pissed at us. Then, in the burn shack, we would light the required number of burners after the mess cook informed us how many they would need for the morning meal and each meal thereafter.

During this time in Vietnam, I continued my bad habit of smoking cigarettes. During one of my afternoon breaks, I was sitting in front of the two 55-gallon drums full of gasoline, which we used to fill the burners. This was covered by a 4' × 8' sheet of plywood so rainwater wouldn't get into the gas cans as we filled them. It rained a lot there because of the humidity. This also acted as a shelter from the sun during the heat of the day. As I sat there, I stupidly lit up a cigarette, smoke billowing from under the plywood. The Executive Officer of the base just happened to be heading to the mess hall for lunch while I was sitting there. He was quite surprised to find me sitting in front of the gas cans, smoking. He called this to my attention and informed me this would be reported and I was not to smoke in this location again. He scared the crap out of me. I thought for sure I would get busted from private first class to private. This never happened. Not sure why.

About two weeks into our mess duty, Richard and I were sitting one evening on our cots, reading mail, when I noticed a Marine enter our tent behind Richard. What I didn't see was the guy behind me. It was a sneak attack on both of us. One guy kicked Richard with his boot right in the face. The other guy started on me. The fight was broken up by others in the mess tent. It seemed that the two Marines were grunt machine gunners (M60s), and we were going to be their replacements on the UH34-D Sikorskys. Because the crew consisted of one crew chief and a gunner, the Marine Corps decided to replace the gunner with a mechanic gunner. That would be us. As a result of this change, the grunts would lose their flight pay each month, and for this, they blamed us! Richard got a busted nose out of this. I wasn't hurt.

Then around the third week into this detail on mess duty, we had one of our daily unexpected fires. In the burn shack, fires were commonplace for us. However, we quickly discovered this day that we had no working fire bottles in the tent. As a consequence, the tent caught fire and was quickly engulfed. I yelled to the mess cook in charge of us to get the large fire bottle (CO_2) out of the mess hall and to call the crash crew. The crash crew was called and quickly arrived and was able to help put out the fire. There was only one man on the fire truck. As he pulled up, I was running through the burn shack, trying to get the recently filled gasoline cans out of the tent, throwing them out one side of the tent, then running back, grabbing two more and running back through. As I ran through the tent the second time, I ran into an Officer, who turned out to be the CO of the base. He said to me, "Take it easy, Marine. We don't want to get anyone hurt."

I responded, "Yes, sir, but the burn shack is next to the food storage tent, and we don't want to lose all the food for the base, sir."

I ran to the crash crew truck and pulled off a fire bottle to help the crash crew driver. The fire was put out. He and I, and no one else, had helped to put out the fire. They had all just stood there watching. I was pissed and looked at my utility shirt to see that my sleeves were burned— luckily, not my arms. I was very lucky, stupid but lucky.

As a consequence of the fire, they had to have an investigation into why it had occurred. Obviously, I was going to be placed on the hot seat because of my previous encounter with the Executive Officer who found me smoking in front of the gas cans. During the investigation, called a Captain's Mass, I also reported that we had to work with an old, non-working compressor. My other comrade in the burn shack reported the same issue with the compressor, as well as the lack of adequate fire bottles in the burn shack. When asked whose responsibility it was, we both reported that it was the responsibility of the mess Sergeant who was in charge of us and the burn shack. The next day after the investigation was completed, we reported to the burn shack for our detail, we not only had a new tent erected but a brand-new electric compressor. We found out later from the base utilities guys that the base had two brand new electric compressors just sitting in storage while we had to use that old piece of crap.

Nothing happened to me after the investigation. I kept my stripe, I was a private first class, but we found out later that the mess Sergeant who was responsible for us got busted one rank. He was an E5 because of what he didn't do in the burn shack, and he was then sent home to the continental United States, which we found to be a little ironic. Thinking back, I would have been lucky to get busted and sent home. Because of this, our last week on mess duty was a bit more pleasant without the mess cook, who was a real asshole. We had a new tent, plenty of fire bottles, and a brand-new compressor, which worked easily, but it didn't help that it was still godawful hot.

When my mess duty time expired a week later, I reported back to my squadron area (HMM-363), and at my first morning formation, I was immediately assigned to aircraft YZ-82. This was very unusual. What usually happened was after their first detail, Marine mechanics were usually assigned to either the hangar deck to work or to their specialty area, such as electronics, avionics, or metal smith. They would not be immediately assigned to a plane, along with flight pay, but it seems that with the smoking issue and the fire, they thought that I was crazy. I'm not sure why.

I reported to the First Sergeant, who told me to find my aircraft on the landing mat. I began looking for my plane. I walked the entire mat and couldn't find my bird. I went back to the Top to report that I couldn't find the plane. They all got a good laugh at my expense. After the ridicule, they told me that the aircraft had in fact been shot down previously and was located on the side of the landing area. So, after finally locating the aircraft, I met the Staff Sergeant assigned with me to the aircraft to refit and repair, so we began to put the bird back together and get it into flight status again.

I found out later that the Staff Sergeant, my first crew chief in country, had just returned from emergency leave for a family issue. He wasn't real happy with being given flight status, as he was a married man with a family back home and was more than happy being assigned to the tool crib or the hangar deck, which is what he was promised once YZ-82 was in flight status again. So we began to repair the plane. We first took the blades off of the bird, as they had multiple bullet holes in them, and put them on a dolly. We dragged them across the flight deck to try to get them replaced, only to be told that they were fine and didn't need replacing. We taped the bullet holes with aviation tape (duct tape). We then brought them back and put them back on the helicopter. Only in Vietnam! This wouldn't have happened in the States. One little ripple in a blade and it's replaced, but three bullet holes? No big deal.

We then rebuilt the transmission, clutch, engine, and tail rotor—my first real experience on a plane that I would fly in. After the plane was placed into flight status, the Staff Sergeant and I were given a mission— nothing as I recall of any consequence, just to make sure she could fly. I was just scared as hell on my first flight in Vietnam, wondering if what we had just done would hold together. And I had an M60 machine gun locked and loaded. I thought to myself, *Now this is getting real.* Everything was fine. The plane flew well except for one complaint (*bitches*, we called them). After each flight pilots would bitch in the flight log about the plane. The pilots reported a beep in the blades, so we put more duct tape on the blades to cover the bullet holes. "Beep fixed," we reported. The duct tape would wear off during every flight.

Shortly after this was completed, the Staff Sergeant was assigned to the tool crib. However, before this he approached me and said are you a Lance Corporal? I said "No" he said I thought you were a Lance Corporal? I put you in for Corporal and was told he couldn't so he put me in for the Lance Corporal stripe. I was then assigned to another aircraft, YZ-64, the plane I would eventually be shot down in, four months later.

Picture of helicopter YZ-64

Sixty-four. This number would and still haunts me to this day. I graduated from high school in the class of 1964. My uncle at this time was a Massachusetts state Representative, and his House seat number was House 64, which was also the license plate number on his car. Today, the license plate number on my car is Disabled Veteran 64. My truck license plate number is Purple Heart 640. I had a motorcycle trike, and its license plate number, assigned at random, was Purple Heart 1046. My Motor Home license plate number is YZ 64.

My eleven-year-old grandson picked number 64 to wear on his all-star uniform two years ago. They won two tournaments in 2017. I was extremely proud of him for his thoughtfulness because I tell him, "That's my lucky number." It turned out to be lucky for him as well. He wears that number still today.

I was assigned this plane, YZ-64, and flew in it from May 1966 until September 15, 1966. We flew every kind of mission. There were VIP missions, transporting dignitaries, military photographers, and high-ranking officers; blood runs and mail runs; troop insertions, both marines and ARVNs (Army of the Republic of Vietnam); search and rescue ops; ammunition runs; and food runs, twenty-four hours a day, seven days a week. The most important mission we flew were the medical evacuations. I had during this period completed more than seventy combat missions and was working on my fourth Air Medal. The Marine Corps at that time awarded an Air Medal for every twenty combat missions, not for VIP or mail runs.

Then on July 1, 1966, my squadron rotated aboard the LPH-5, the USS *Princeton* helicopter carrier from Ky-Ha in South Vietnam to begin operations at the DMZ (demilitarized zone). This was to be a temporary rotation, as the *Princeton* was about to rotate back to CONUS (Continental United States) as they had completed their tour of duty (spanning thirteen months) in Vietnam. During our time on the *Princeton*, we had a mission in the Saigon area, where we brought in a Marine unit fresh from the States to an area in the south. After only one day, we found ourselves bringing in planeloads of jerry cans full of water. Then we went in to bring them back to the ship. The next day, they had one wounded and one KIA, and they saw no un-friendlies in the area. They were shooting at each other. These kids were more frightened than I was.

In the middle of July1966, we were transferred from the LPH-5 to the LPH-2, the USS *Iwo Jima*. Below is a picture of me sitting in the door with my M60 machine gun.

Picture of me in door of helicopter with M60 machine gun

The Marines from the 1st Battalion, 26th Marines, on the *Princeton* were combined with the 3rd Battalion, 26th Marines, on the *Iwo Jima*. I remember an incident aboard the *Iwo Jima*. After a late mission in country, as we landed late aboard the flight deck and because we were last in, we were required to tie down on the flight deck. During the evening, the Navy made popcorn in the hangar deck for the ship's movie each night. Their popcorn was limited to a certain number of bags per night, so everyone got in line to get popcorn. Needless to say, my crew chief and I were at the end of the line this night when a grunt Sergeant walked back to us. You could tell who the wing wipers were as we wore our .38 pistols backward, John Wayne style. We were dirty from grease and oil and fuel spills. Our brass was dirty, and our boots weren't polished. The grunts hated us—at least some did.

The Sergeant who approached us said, "You guys air wing?"

"Yes," we replied.

"Come up here with me. You were the guys who pulled us out today."

He was near the head of the line. I said to him, "Look, these guys will want to kill us if we cut the line."

He said, "Don't worry about them," so we proceeded to follow him and cut the line—not without a few choice words directed at us. The Sergeant stopped, turned to them, and said, "Look, these men are Marines. They're air wing. When you are in country and need ammunition, food, or water or if you need to be medevacked, these are the guys who are going to get your ass out of the shit." Not another word was said, and we both got our popcorn, which was a treat for us.

While aboard these two helicopter carriers, we pulled missions from Saigon to the DMZ and steamed twice to the NAS (Naval Air Station) Subic Bay in the Philippines to replenish the ship stores for food and supplies and to do maintenance and pick up replacement helicopters for our squadron, as well as grunt Marines (infantry) to replace those lost in action in Vietnam. On the USS *Iwo Jima*, they were the 3rd Battalion, 26th Marine Detachment. During the next few months, we performed many missions, sometimes at night doing medivacs or daily troop insertions or equipment, munitions, food, or water runs. During this time, I did more than ninety combat missions, twenty-five in one five-day period from July 22 to the 27 of 1966. This was exhausting. Here I was able to get my first picture taken with my aircrew wings, ribbons and expert rifle badge, and Lance Corporal stripe before I was wounded.

Picture of me at Subic Bay, Phillipines

My memory of those days fades on occasion. One memory that haunts me is of a particular medivac we had at night. The pitch black darkness of Vietnam at night was unforgettable. We flew to the coordinates given to us. When we approached what we thought was the location, the pilot turned on the helicopter light. Now we were a sitting duck for any enemy out there. But we spotted the grunts and proceeded to land. We took the wounded Marine into the plane. He had no trousers on and was naked from the waist down. He used his trousers as a pillow. I leaned down and asked where he was hit. He said, "They shot my balls off." He had taken a hit to his nuts. What a mess. We could do nothing for him, as we had no Corpsman with us; in fact, we never had a Corpsman on any medivac that I did. As we flew him back to the aircraft carrier, I looked down at him. He was smiling. I realized he was looking at the ceiling of the plane, where I had taped a few *Playboy* centerfold pictures. I was pleased that I had done that for that reason.

Once, during the daytime mission, we were asked along with three other planes to do a body recovery mission, as a number of Marines had been killed by friendly fire—short rounds fired from an American ship offshore. We removed eight planeloads of Marines that day, all in body bags. It was horrible. Picking up the bags was heartbreaking, as some, we could tell, were just body parts. My plane was the last in that day. Our second flight, we removed all the weapons these Marines had been carrying. We filled the plane. It was a mountain of M14s, M60s, M1s, and shotguns. Then they threw the gunny sack on the plane. The crew chief and I looked at each other, curious as to what was in the bag, so I opened it. It was full of .45 caliber pistols, so I took two of them for us to have in the plane. They were all dirty and muddy, with that red clay all over them.

We were now operating off the coast of South Vietnam, in the South China Sea near the DMZ (Demilitarized Zone) in the Quang Tri Province of Vietnam. HMM-363 (Marine Medium Helicopter Squadron-363) was known as the "Lucky Red Lions." On this particular morning of September 15, 1966, I awoke to the remnants of a monsoon that had struck during the previous evening, leaving my bird YZ-64 (Yankee Zulu-64) on the flight deck, soaked with water. The morning began just like many others—warm but damp and humid because of the rains. I found that our flak jackets we had left in the plane overnight the day before to be soaked from the rains because our plane leaked like a sieve, so I removed them from the plane and laid them on the flight deck to dry before our mission that morning.

As we prepared for the beginning of operation "Deckhouse IV," a new co-pilot appeared on the flight deck to co-pilot my plane. He and I proceeded to preflight the bird. During the preflight, the co-pilot, who was wearing an international orange-colored flight suit, began to ream my ass for having belts of ammo for my M60 machine gun hanging from the radio cable inside the helicopter, right next to my window. I tried to explain to the new former "jet jockey" that we had had a problem just a few weeks earlier with access to ammo when we were confronted with enemy fire. But he wasn't having any of it. He seemed to be enjoying the ass-reaming he was giving me. He then found I had taped the April 1966 *Playboy* centerfolds to the ceiling of the helicopter and also that some of my safety wire in the engine compartment was not tight enough for him.

As he was performing this ream job, the pilot also arrived on deck the flight deck in time to hear the reaming. He abruptly stepped in, saying to me, "Good morning, DJ."

I responded, "Good morning, Sir."

He said, "Is the plane ready."

"Yes, Sir," I replied.

"Why don't you go do something while I speak with the Lieutenant," he said.

"Yes, sir," I replied, and I went around to the other side of the plane, where I could hear every word of their conversation. The pilot had recently been promoted to full-bird Colonel and wasn't even supposed to fly missions any longer, but he wanted one more until he received his "eagles." He was a great guy. I wish I could remember his name. He began to ream the Lieutenant, first by questioning his "orange" fly suit. He then said, "This plane has the most flight hours in the squadron every month. That's because this crew works very hard to keep it in good flying shape. They fix the plane they fly in, so unless you find something dangerous, get off their back. As far as the ammo is concerned, if we get into trouble, these are the guys who are going to bail our ass out, so let's go."

The Lieutenant replied, "Yes, Sir."

The Colonel also ordered the Lieutenant to change his flight suit before we left. The Colonel then called me and said, "Is she ready to fly?"

I said, "Yes, Sir."

"Good, let's go."

When the preflight was finally completed with the Colonel, we closed the clam shell compartment and we took off on our primary mission, which was a troop insertion and assault at the DMZ. Our plane was rated as one of the top planes for flight hours completed for the last three months, averaging over ninety flight hours per month for that period.

We flew off of the LPH-2 to the DMZ in South Vietnam with grunts from the 3rd batallion 26 th Marines off the *Iwo* for our assigned Deckhouse IV mission. The primary mission that day was initially uneventful. We brought in Marine grunts without incident, although we were told before the flight that there were enemy troops in the area and it may be a "HOT" zone. Our rules of engagement at that time were not to fire unless fired upon. We received no enemy fire. Everything was eerie and quiet. After lifting off from the primary LZ (landing zone), we were immediately called on our radio to a secondary mission, which was an emergency medivac and extraction. The report we received was that there were thirteen marine recon that needed immediate assistance, with two reported KIAs (killed in action) and two WIAs (wounded in action). As we approached the coordinates we were given, we spotted the grunts. These recon Marines had been inserted the day before and were ambushed by North Vietnam regulars. They were pinned down and were running out of ammunition.

I felt immediately that we were in trouble, as we were flying in at treetop level into what we knew was a HOT zone. We were in the Quang Tri Province (with un-friendlies in the area). This was not SOP (standard operating procedure). I was told later that the left seat (co-pilot) had the controls and the Colonel was navigating his approach after given the new coordinates, which again had us flying at treetop level. I remember thinking that this was like coming into Logan Airport, in Boston. The enemy could hear and see us coming from miles away. We were sitting ducks, but the door gunner and I were both at the ready.

Our normal approach would be to come in at altitude, then pull an autorotation into the landing zone. During this approach, we disengage the main rotor head from the engine centrifugal force. This keeps the blades spinning, but the engine is throttled down so we go in a little quieter then as we get near the ground. We reengage the main rotor head and throttle up. This is when you see the helicopter flare up and land—a much safer, quieter, and softer approach, but on this day, this mission, we didn't do that. I don't blame anyone. My feeling is "shit happens."

As we approached the LZ, I saw the shot that they say you never hear. I saw the dirt kicking up from the ground from what was later discovered to be a 30-caliber machine gun. I also saw tracer rounds coming toward me, all this happening in a split second. To my shock, I was struck. The first round had hit me in the chin and neck. The second round struck me in the right chest. The two rounds came right up the barrel of my M60 machine gun, which was in my right shoulder, with my hand in the trigger housing and my finger on the trigger.

I was later told that the plane took four hits all together; the first went through the clutch, the second went behind the left seat (co-pilot), severing the three throttle linkages in the center console but not breaking them. The next two rounds went through the left side forward window, both of them striking me—one hell of a shot.

To this day, I remain amazed, not so much at the shot but rather that I'm still here and able to tell my story.

Russ and me in front of YZ 64 on the USS Iwo Jima

I was also told a few days later by "Russ," my crew chief that day, that the machine gun used was a 30-caliber air-cooled machine gun, one of ours that the NVA (North Vietnamese Army) had captured and used against us. We did recapture the machine gun and took two NVA prisoners that day. I was told because the Marines ran out of ammo that it was hand-to-hand combat. All our Marines were extracted from the zone.

When I was struck, I immediately lost the use of my right arm. I remember standing in the plane at the window I was flying that day. As the first mechanic approaching the LZ I was at the ready, with my machine gun locked and loaded, my left foot was up on my seat and my right hand was on the trigger. The seats we had in the belly of the plane for the door gunner and the window gunner were previously Huey gunship pilot seats. We came across these seats from a chopper that had been shot down, so we cannibalized the seats and installed them in our plane for the crew to sit on. We previously sat on aluminum fold-down sling seats, on which we put a case of C-rations to sit on so we could be a little higher in the seat for our machine guns.

As I said before, I watched the round that struck me come right up the muzzle of my machine gun. When it hit me, it threw my right arm back, throwing me off balance, at which time I fell to the deck (floor) of the aircraft. I knew I was hit but thought this couldn't be that bad because I could see no blood, so I tried to get up. Because I was wearing my flight helmet, I was unable to turn my head to see anything. Every time I tried and turned my head, it turned into the helmet.

I tried to feel my right arm with my left hand, but I had my flight gloves. I could feel nothing. Looking at my left gloved hand, I could see no blood, so I tried to stand up again. All this probably happened within just a few seconds, but it felt like an eternity. Suddenly, my breathing got very difficult. I felt as if someone were sitting on my chest. It was also godawful hot, but still, I couldn't see any blood or any reason for my situation—that is, being on the floor of the bird, flat on my back. What the hell was going on?

I then realized as I fell to the floor that I had become disconnected from my helmet ICS (internal communication system) radio, and I was therefore unable to communicate with any of the flight crew. I was trying to call them and tell them I that I thought I had been hit.

As I looked over to my crew chief, Corporal Russell "Russ,", who was in the door gunner position. I realized he was returning machine-gun fire from his M60 and was himself very busy, so I decided simply to lie there and wait. I remember thinking, *This is it. The war's over for me, but I'm not going to die in this godawful, smelly, hot country, not like this.* So I started breathing very slowly. Then I saw Russ looking over at my location, at least to where I should have been standing. Not seeing me at first at the window, he looked down and saw me lying on the deck. I saw his face turn white. I thought he was looking at a ghost.

He was a guy with pale sunburned skin and reddish hair. Looking at me, he turned as white as a sheet. I saw his hand go to his helmet's radio mouthpiece. We had to press our hand to the mouthpiece so the pilots could hear us because of the noise in the belly of the plane. He notified the pilots of my situation, as they were unaware at that time that we had been hit and were proceeding down to the LZ. We were the lead plane on this medivac mission and had three other UH-34D Sikorsky helicopters with us. As Russ radioed the pilots, I could feel the plane begin lifting up and gaining altitude. It was a great feeling to know we were not landing. Knowing we were no longer going into a hot zone with me on my back gave me some relief.

Russ would later tell me that he had heard and saw me firing first. Then, within seconds, he started to receive fire from his side of the helicopter. Then, after a few seconds, he realized I was no longer firing my machine gun. As he turned to see what was happening with me, he saw my machine gun hanging out the side window, and I wasn't there. Looking down, he saw me lying on the deck with blood everywhere. The rounds that hit me had gone right through me and through the other side of the aircraft.

After Russ radioed the pilots of my situation, he then unplugged his radio and came over to help me, the first thing was to plug his helmet into my radio jack so he could communicate with the pilots from my position. He seemed shocked and didn't seem to know what to do for me at first. Today, I still feel bad for Russ, and I would like to reconnect with him to thank him for saving my life.

Not seeing anything wrong myself, I wasn't worried, not yet anyway. My head was at the rear radio compartment facing the front of the aircraft, and above my head, mounted to the bulkhead of the plane, was the first-aid kit. I pointed with my left hand to the first-aid kit, thinking I had been hit somewhere but not knowing how badly. I was more than likely bleeding, I reasoned.

Russ immediately pulled the first-aid kit from the bulkhead, but because it had rained the night before, water had collected behind the kit and came pouring out from behind the first-aid pouch right into my face. I remember thinking, *Boy, that sure felt good.* Russ then took my flight helmet off and placed a compress around my chin. Seeing the wound on my chin, he thought I had been shot in the jaw. I must have been a sight to see.

Thank God for the outstanding pilots, squadron crewmembers, corpsmen, and ship's crew as the helicopter headed back to the *Iwo Jima* so we could access the medical/surgical unit aboard the ship. As we approached, I felt the plane descending to land on the flight deck. What a great feeling. However, as we started our approach to land, I felt the plane start shaking violently. The pilot stopped his descent and lifted off without touching down. He then went around for another attempt to land. I saw Russ go to his mouthpiece again. He later told me he had radioed the pilot with the urgency of my situation, telling him we must land this time or I was going to bleed to death. On the second attempt, the plane again began to shake. Again, this time, the pilot pushed the collective control down hard, slamming the struts into the flight deck with a hard landing.

They immediately shut the engine and rotor head down. The engine then caught on fire the crash crew (firefighters) aboard the ship, putting the fire out by blowing CO_2 down the exhaust port of the engine. What a shame. It was such a great bird. Russ told me later that this was reportedly caused by the 30-caliber hit to the clutch assembly, which caused it to disintegrate during our flight over the South China Sea to the *Iwo Jima*. I have often thought, *What if we went down into the sea?* I never would have survived. Thank God for the pilots that day.

As all this was going on with the crash landing and the engine fire, a corpsman, again whose name I also don't know, jumped into the plane to attend to me. He took one look at my wounds and the dressing Russ had placed on my chin and immediately moved the dressing to my neck wound, which was opened to about two inches and bleeding profusely. He I'm sure thought that was the major injury to the neck.

It's funny the things that go through your mind. I remember thinking back to the first-aid class at Camp Lejeune in California, which I had attended in March. A marine had asked, "Where do you put the compress when it's a neck wound?" and the instructor said, "Around the neck, and press tightly." We all laughed, thinking, *You'll choke the poor bastard*, and here I was, the poor bastard. Without any further hesitation, the corpsman reached under me with both arms.

From the squat position, he picked me up, turned, and placed me on the waiting stretcher. I remember being impressed by this feat. Even in the state I was in, I was acutely aware of everything happening around me. I was impressed because, at the time, I weighed in at a solid 182 pounds, no lightweight.

Then four stretcher-bearers ran me across the flight deck toward the helicopter elevator, which was used to bring helicopters up from the hangar deck to the flight deck, to take me below to the hangar deck to the waiting surgical triage team. While we were running across the flight deck, I remember screaming in pain because my right arm had fallen off the stretcher. As it was hanging down, it hurt something awful. The corpsman who had lifted me was running alongside of me. I yelled to the corpsmen to stop, so they put me down, and he asked me what was wrong. I told him my arm hurt. He lifted my right arm, raising it over my chest, and let the arm go, not realizing it was useless. It fell to my chest. I thought, *I can't feel my hand, and I can't control it.*

I grunted when it hit my chest, again not realizing that the bullet had broken three ribs on my right side and that my lung had collapsed. They picked me up again, continuing on to the elevator. As we descended on the elevator to the hangar deck, the elevator began to jump, causing me to begin to worry again. This had happened to me before but not while I was lying on my back in the middle of the elevator floor.

Just a few weeks earlier, we had been bringing my helicopter up the elevator to the flight deck. The SOP (standard operating procedure) in case a tie down broke loose or in the case of the hydraulic elevator, if there was air in the line and it began to jump, the crewman was there to push the breaks hard so the helicopter wouldn't jump over the side of the ship. Sure as hell, one day, this happened to me. While in the plane on the elevator, air in the line caused the elevator to jump twice. I thought I would shit my pants. That would have been quite a fall from the flight deck to the South China Sea below, but that didn't happen. It was just air in the line.

The stretcher-bearers and I made it down the elevator to the hangar deck, and they carried me over to the medical triage team who were waiting for me so they could evaluate my condition. My stretcher was then placed over two wooden sawhorses. I thought, *This is really crazy.*

Wooden saw horses? They began to remove my sidearm a .38-caliber pistol, my survival knife, pistol belt, flight gloves, and six rounds of ammunition I had placed in every pocket of my jungle fatigues (which, as I remember, had ten pockets). I remember hearing a corpsman say, "This guy's a walking armory." My pistol belt was the only one in the squadron with a twenty-round bandolier on it, and I had placed six .38-caliber rounds in each pocket of my jungle utilities, anticipating that if I was shot down, I would have plenty of ammo on me at least.

After cutting off all my clothes and baring me naked, they seemed to have trouble determining exactly what was wrong with me. They took the compress off my neck and saw nothing but a gash in my right neck, about two inches across, and a cut on my right chin, but neither was a through-and-through wound. I started to complain again because my right arm had fallen off of the stretcher once again during all the clothing removal, and it was pulling on my right side, which still hurt like hell. The doctor treating me asked me what was wrong. I said, "My right arm hurts," so he too picked it up held it above my chest, once again letting it go, dropping it to my chest for the second time. It fell off the stretcher yet again. I started to get agitated and complained about my back hurting me. The doctor said, "Roll him over." They rolled me over onto my left side to look at my back.

That's when they discovered that the small hole in my right chest, which they hadn't seen with all the blood, was in fact the entrance gunshot wound, which had gone through and through, exiting out my right back. The hole in the front was the size of a fingertip. The exit wound was about three inches in diameter, located on my right clavicle bone.

The doctor didn't hesitate. He ordered the corpsmen to get me up to surgery, stat. I was then lifted up on the stretcher by two corpsmen, this while I was naked and bleeding. They placed the stretcher onto the tongues of a forklift that was waiting in the hangar deck. The forklift was then driven over to an area in the hangar deck, where two more corpsman were waiting up on the next level up in the ship. I would be lifted into sick bay, where the surgical team was waiting.

I must admit, while I was being lifted the fifteen or so feet up, I was, for the first time that day, at that moment, a bit scared that after all this, they would drop me right on my head. Luckily, that didn't happen. I remember the two corpsmen stepping out onto the two tongues of the forklift, grabbing the stretcher, and lifting me through the sick bay door. I was transferred onto a freezing metal table. This turned out to be an X-ray table, where they took pictures and discovered that my right lung had collapsed and the top three ribs on my right side were, in fact, broken.

The next thing I remember, the flight surgeon was looking down at me, asking, "Where you from, marine?"

I said, "Massachusetts, sir"

"Where about in Massachusetts?"

"New Bedford."

"That's great. I did my internship at Mass General in Boston."

An Asian (Chinese) corpsman was shaving what little hair I had on my chest. I was concerned because for the past few months while in Vietnam, I'd had a heat rash on my chest, and this guy was shaving my chest with the one and only chest hair I had grown. At this time, I also questioned the surgical attendant as we to were fighting what we called the "gooks," and here I was having one shave my chest. I don't feel I am a bigot, but that was how I felt then. I feel differently about the Vietnamese Americans as well as other Asians I've met today.

I had a visit from the squadron priest, who was there to give me the last rites. God, that wasn't a good feeling. Now I was worried. I kept thinking, *This isn't going to happen to me, not here.* The last thing I remember was the flight surgeon up on the surgical table above me, pushing some kind of rod into my chest. As he leaned over me and began to push, I grunted from the pressure on my chest. He stopped suddenly and asked, "Did you feel that?" Before I could answer, someone said to count backward from one hundred. I started to respond and got to ninety-nine, and then I was out like a light.

The surgery went as well as could be expected. They saved my life, which is a good thing. They did it by performing a right thoracotomy, which is the surgical splitting open of my right chest. They opened me up from my right nipple around to the center of my back. After they completed the repairs to my chest, removing the three broken pieces of ribs, repairing the collapsed lung, and stopping the bleeders, they inserted a chest tube into my right lung through the chest wall to drain my right lung.

When I woke up the next day, I found myself lying in a hospital bed. I could hear talking in the room and awakened to discover a doctor talking to a navy chief petty officer from the engineering department aboard the ship. They were pointing under my bed. After they left, the marine in the bottom bunk next to me said, "They didn't think you were going to make it." He later told me that the navy chief had been asked to jury rig a pump to suction the fluid from my chest, as the surgical team aboard the *Iwo* didn't have a suction pump available. The pump worked just fine, and everyone seemed to be pleased with the results, especially me.

There were two marines next to me in the two bunks in sickbay. I remember being told that they were the two marines we went in to pull out. They were both wounded. They both seemed to be in better shape than me. The guy on the bottom bunk had fair skin and had reddish hair. He and I would relive this chance meeting of sorts some seven years later, when we would find each other once again. Now, fifty-four years later, that grunt Marine (George H) and I are friends again, living only a few miles apart from each other. *Semper fi* (always faithful) may be just words to some people, but to a Marine it's forever.

On the second day in sick bay, the priest came in again to give me the last rites for a second time. I was now very angry and swore at him.

"Get the fuck out of here!"

I felt bad about that later, but I was fighting to live, and this was the second time I saw him. Later that day, my crew chief, Russ, stopped by to visit. He was with General Lewis Walt, the commanding general of marines in Vietnam at the time. It seems Russ stopped him on his visit to the ship and asked if he would present to me my combat air crewman wings, which I had earned but had not yet been awarded because we were a bit busy with the fighting and all. Russ asked General Walt to give me his personal wings. The general agreed and came into sickbay. I remember this vaguely, as I was a bit drugged up, but I do remember the visit as if it were yesterday.

He took the wings that Russ had given him and pinned them to my pillow. He also pinned a Purple Heart medal to my pillow. He pinned

Purple Hearts to the other two marines in sickbay with me that day as well. General Walt would one day become the commandant of the Marine Corps. This would be the last time I remember seeing Russ, my friend. I wish I knew what happened to him. He's not on the Vietnam Wall.

Chapter 11

Hospital Ship Repose

On day three on the *Iwo Jima*, I awoke to find the Corpsman preparing me for a helicopter ride. They were transferring me to the Hospital Ship USS *Repose*, which was at that time operating off the coast of South Vietnam, where the surgical team that operated on me on the *Iowa Jima* had come from. They brought me up to the flight deck, put me on an HMM-363 helicopter, and flew me to the *Repose*. This would be, I thought, the last time I would see a UH-34D helicopter from my squadron.

The short flight was uneventful. We landed aboard the hospital ship, and I was immediately taken to a ward where they hooked my chest tube up to another real suction machine. The pain was unbelievable. My right arm was in excruciating pain. I was given the painkiller Demerol, by injection. This continued every four hours, te relief, although short-lived (three to four hours), was great. I tried to make the shot last as long as I possibly could. Eight to ten hours was all I could do.

The surgeon aboard the *Repose*, Dr. William Stewart, had told me to ask for it whenever I needed it but try not to ask if I wasn't having pain. After a few days lying on my back, they decided to change the sheet on my bunk. This meant they had to get me up. As I sat on the edge of the bunk, I looked back at the sheet I had been lying on. To my shock, the sheet was covered in dried blood. Worst of all, it was mine.

What the hell was going on? The Nurses and Corpsmen assured me that everything was okay; it seemed that the exit wound in my back had been left open to drain and to heal a bit on its own before they attempted to close it surgically. Because I didn't have access to a mirror, I wasn't able to see the extent of the wound in my back, and with all the pain I had, I didn't know whether the arm, the chest, or the back hurt the most, except I knew now there was a hole in my back. It was not a small amount of blood.

Approximately three weeks later, the doctor came to my bedside to tell me it was time to remove my chest tube. I was grateful to hear this, as I hated using bedpans and wanted to be able to walk to the head (toilet) on my own. As the doctor sat there waiting for assistance from one of the very busy Corpsmen and Nurses, another Marine patient on the ward walked by and said, "Hey, Doc, need some help?"

The Doctor replied, "Yes, I do. Come over here."

The patient was shocked when he was asked to pull the chest tube out of me as the Doctor held a gauze pad over the opening in my right chest.

The Doctor told the Marine, "When I tell you to, pull. Just pull straight and quickly." The Marine did as he was told, and the tube came out easily, without any discomfort. As he was pulling it, it looked as if it was four feet long and was very gross. Just as the tube cleared my chest, I heard what sounded like air being released from a balloon. As I heard this, the doctor quickly pressed gauze over the opening. He held it for a while and then gave me a couple of stitches, and that was it. The tube was out, and I was free from the suction machine after four weeks. More importantly, I was now able to get up and walk to the toilet on my own.

Shortly after this episode, I called for help to get up. I found with my right arm now in a sling, it was difficult to get up from the prone position with this dead weight on my chest, which was my right arm. I had to get out on my right side. Because of this, they changed me to another bed where I could get out by pushing off on my left side. Now I got out of my rack and proceeded to the head. As I walked through the ward, I noticed all kinds of injuries and wounds. As I approached the head, just to my left was a Filipino marine with burns all over his body. Face to feet, everything you could see was burned. As I found later, he was burned with gasoline. As I passed him with the Corpsman attending to him, I had to stop and watch as the Corpsman poured saline solution over his dressings, then proceeded to peel the wet dressing from him, peeling a thin layer of skin with the hopes to regenerate new skin. The Filipino just lay there, saying nothing at all, just looking at me as I looked at him.

**Picture on the USS *Repose* with me, unknown
Marine and the Filipino marine**

During my first trip to the head, I had to look into the mirror, and as I did, others were just looking at me as I looked over my shoulder to see the hole in my back. Wow! I thought what a mess I was. That was my real first look at myself. I also noticed the tremendous weight loss from over 160 pounds before I was hit to a mere 130 pounds. I looked like a skeleton.

It was now the middle of October 1966, and the doctors were trying to decide what to do with me next, as they didn't like to operate on guys very often because of the rate of infection, unless it was a matter of life or death. They decided to operate on me, and that would occur around the middle of October, one month after my initial gunshot wound. The operation was an attempt to repair the damage to my right arm by repairing the damage done by the bullet. I remember them giving me medication that morning, which knocked me on my ass. I awakened in pre-op, looking up at the clock, then passed out again from the drugs they gave me.

A short while later, I found myself back, in my rack on the Orthopedic ward. As I lay there, I could see a lot of bandages on my right shoulder. I awakened to see Doctor Stewart sitting on my left side with his arms on the right side of my rack, leaning over me. I knew in my heart that things hadn't gone well, as a very brief time had passed between pre-op and now. The Doctor began to explain to me what they had done and what they found.

Unfortunately, to get to the gunshot damaged area they had to surgically break my right shoulder. After this, they found I had only one nerve that was not damaged by the bullet, and that was the nerve that transmitted the pain signal from my brain to my right arm. As a result, they were not able to fix the damage. During this conversation, I asked the doctor what had happened to me. We sat for what seemed like a long time as he explained that the round that did all the damage came up from the ground, hit me, in what is called the right brachial plexus area of my right chest. It hit me, it then traveled downward, hit the right top three ribs in my chest, then went through the top lobe of my right lung, exiting out my back.

When the bullet exited my back, it traveled inexplicably around my right shoulder blade, one of the largest and thinnest bones in the human body, without breaking it. To this day, the scar on my back amazes me. It was during this conversation that Doctor Stewart said, "Dan, you'll probably never get the use of your arm back again." As he said this to me, I could feel the sincerity in his voice and could see the tears in his eyes. I began to cry as well. This was devastating news for a man at the ripe old age of twenty. I was in the best shape of my life before this incident. What would I do now? He gave me yet another shot to sedate me and left me alone. Shortly after, I awakened to a determination that "they" weren't going to get me. I would live and live well if I could just get out of this damn place.

The next thing they recommended on the ship was physical therapy to stretch my right arm out. The corpsman therapist on my first visit tried to extend my arm over my head. I told him I couldn't move the arm myself and that it was very painful. He seemed not to care and stretched my arm over my head, tearing my right chest (pectoral) muscle, which added to my pain. I screamed and swore at him, telling him how much he had hurt me. They took me back to my ward and gave me my medication, asking what had happened. After telling them what he had done, they discovered that my right pectoral muscle was torn. I found out later that the corpsman in PT was sent to Vietnam as a grunt corpsman. This created yet another problem for me.

Now the issue was the pain in my arm. Doctor Stewart wanted to try what they called "nerve blocks." This is where they numb you—in my case, the right clavicle area near the entry wound. The doctors found it amazing that I was still alive, as the bullet that did all the damage went between by jugular vein and my right clavicle bone. One inch either way would have killed me for sure. This is where even more ironies come into play.

One day before the first nerve block and after I was taken off the suction machine one of the Red Lucky Lions, UH-34Ds from my squadron stopped by to see how I was doing. I was able to go outside the ward to see the plane on the *Repose's* flight deck. While up there, one of my crew chiefs, Bob M, was crewing the plane, so I asked him to help me to try on his flak vest. I'm still in touch with Bob to this day. He went on to earn two Bronze Stars for valor and numerous other air medals and awards.

Picture of Bob M and myself on the LPH 2

Back then our flak vests were designed with a ringed collar made of a plastic material, which, in my case, rode right on my clavicle bone. Later, I would be told by the doctors that had I been wearing my flak vest that morning. Because the rounds came up at me from the ground, the chances were more than likely that if they had hit the vest, the vest might have deflected the rounds upward under my chin and through my head, which would have been the end of me. To this day, I feel very fortunate that it rained that morning and I had forgotten our vests on the flight deck.

Back to the nerve-block issue, Dr. Stewart came to me one day to tell me what he was going to try, with my permission. I was willing to do whatever it took to stop the pain. The purpose of the nerve block, as it was explained to me, was to deaden the nerve that was transmitting the pain signal from by brain to my right arm. The process began by laying me on a table and spreading this godawful reddish-black betadine solution all over my right jaw and neck area. What a mess, and this stuff doesn't come off easily. The doctor then loaded a very long needle— without exaggeration, it was at least four inches long—with Novocain to deaden the area of my right chest that they were going into. They then proceeded down through my neck with the needle to find the nerve in my right shoulder that was causing me pain.

When they hit the spot they were seeking, I asked how they knew when they hit the right nerve. The doctor said when my pupils dilated, then they had it. He removed the syringe from the needle, leaving the needle in me and refilling the syringe with another substance, called Carbocane. He then reattached the syringe to the needle in my chest. Finding the right nerve, he injected God knows how many cubic centimeters of Carbocane into the nerve in my neck. The good thing for me was it worked, at least for a while. The pain went away, but the side effect of this treatment was blindness. That's right, I couldn't see a damn thing—totally blind.

After two of these treatments, I said no way in hell was I going to do this again. The doctor then said to me, "If anyone ever tries to do a nerve block on you again, make sure they don't use alcohol." He said if they wanted to use alcohol, they might as well put a .45 to my head and blow it off. Nerve blocks would be tried again a few months later, back in the States, with the same results.

During my time aboard the *Repose*, I was notified that my oldest sister was going to get married at the end of November of 1966, on Thanksgiving Day. Realizing this and believing that I probably wouldn't make it home in time for the wedding, I thought the least I could do was to send a wedding present back home. The problem with this was how would I find something aboard the *Repose*? Others aboard the ship told me the ship exchange was below deck and carried a variety of stuff. So one day, after getting my much-needed narcotic injection, I left the ward without telling anyone where I was headed and preceded below deck, down the stairwell, to the ship exchange. This was probably four or five flights of stairs, but it felt like forty or fifty. After a long and tiring walk down to the ship's store, I discovered they had a sterling silverware set, so I bought it. I think it cost me $30.00 American. I said I'd take it with me back up to the ward. Remember, no elevators, a fifty-pound weight loss for me, along with four weeks of lying on my back, countless drugs, and one functioning lung. And the heat,God, it was so very hot.

Well, I didn't make it back to the ward. I was found by some sailors passed out in one of the stairwells and was taken back to my ward. I was awakened with a corpsman asking me, "What the hell were you thinking?"

I replied, "My sister is getting married next month. Chances are, I won't be there, and I wanted to get her something."

"Look, don't ever do that again. Why don't you give me your sister's name and address, and I'll mail it home for you?" I gave him my parents address in New Bedford. He looked at me and said "What?"

I said, "Is that a problem?"

He said, "No, I live in Fall River."

We exchanged addresses and promised to look each other up upon our return home. Regrettably, this corpsman and I would meet again years later under opposite circumstances.

It was now the end of October 1966, around October 25. I'd been on the *Repose* for over a month, and they were getting ready to medivac some of us to CONUS (Continental United States). The plan was to fly us by helicopter to the DMZ in Vietnam. Then a C130 Air Force transport plane would pick us up and fly us to the Naval Hospital in Agana, Guam. I asked the Corpsmen if I could walk, but the Nurses and Doctors insisted that it would best if I was listed as non-ambulatory patient. They were right.

Chapter 12

The Trip Home

The trip from the hospital ship *Repose* was traumatic, especially when I was told that we were flying back to Vietnam by helicopter to the DMZ. I got a bit concerned, to say the least. A shot of Demerol was in order. It was at night, which is dark as hell there. They have no street lights, no house lights, unbelievably dark in Vietnam, total blackness.

Now, here I am totally helpless and without a weapon. Not that I could have used it in my condition anyway. We flew by helicopter to the DMZ, where we were loaded onto an Air Force C130 transport plane and flown out, thankfully without incident. The flight Nurses were terrific. If you groaned or moved, they were there with an injection. *Wow,* talk about high. We eventually landed at NAS, Agana, Guam, where I was to stay for a week. While there, the Marine Gunnery Sergeant in charge gathered all the Marines that were there for a pep talk under the assumption that we were all going back into combat and we needed to square ourselves away—meaning get haircuts, new uniforms, etc. As frustrated as I was, I had to speak up at that time. To say the least, I was very bitter. I said to the Gunny, "If you think I'm getting a haircut, you are out of your mind. All I'm doing is going home."

The Gunny looked at me, realizing it was a mistake to have me at this meeting. He said nothing in response, just looked at me and my arm and said, "I'm sorry."

I went back to my rack.

It was awfully hot and humid in Guam, just as it was in Vietnam. It would be extremely humid, so much so that it would rain, then get even more humid. It never changed. I was still getting the Demerol every four to six hours, as needed, but then, while at the naval hospital, they tried to take the pressure off of my right shoulder by putting my right arm in a full cast. I had a picture taken of me in bed with the cast on.

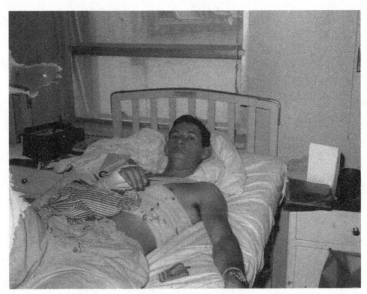

**Picture of me in hospital bed with a cast on my
arm in Agana, Guam, Naval Hospital.**

This was awful, a full arm cast on an arm that I couldn't hold up, with a sling over my right shoulder where I'd just had a gunshot wound and recent surgery. It made no sense to me, and it didn't work. Instead, my right shoulder's surgical site opened up a bit and began to ooze this lovely green puss. Yep, it got infected as the surgical scar opened up and the sweat and other microorganisms got in. So now I'm on antibiotics to try to stop the green shit from coming out of the surgical scar. They finally smartened up and removed the cast from my arm as well. I have pictures of me wearing this stupid cast. Unbelievable. I didn't receive any new uniforms for my trip home, but I did get a haircut.

Now we're boarding yet another plane after a week on this lovely island for my next stop on the long trip home. The next stop was Manila in the Philippines. This was going to be another life experience for me. We landed during the afternoon, originally to stay for a short time to refuel and then fly onto California, but it seems that President Lyndon B. Johnson was visiting Manila on his way to visit the troops in Vietnam, and because of this, no flights were either coming into or leaving Manila. So here I was, stuck in Manila. The problem was they put me, the only American, up in an old wooden army hospital barracks with four Filipino marines none of whom spoke a word of English.

I had a lot of respect for Filipino marines, but these guys completely ignored me. I also found out that there is a difference—at least, there was back in the 60s – between the army medics' and navy/marine corpsmen's ability to treat the wounded. Army medics, for example, cannot dispense narcotics, so here I was, all alone, with no one who spoke my language and no medic or nurse in sight to hear my yelling and screaming. Remember now, we had no call buzzers, no telephones, no way to call for assistance. My four Filipino roommates were more concerned with their newly purchased stereo equipment they had picked up in Vietnam than they were with my problems.

Eventually, a medic arrived to check on me and told me the story about the nurse coming to see me as soon as he passed the word. Evidently, they weren't prepared to handle the troops coming through their hospital. I was amazed and very pissed off. I was there for two days, which were mostly a blur for me. We then boarded yet another C130 transport for the trip home at last—or so I thought.

Our first stop was in Hawaii. When the rear door opened, a navy admiral came aboard to welcome us home. Everyone on the C130 on stretchers booed him and asked him not very nicely to get out. Our next stop was in CONUS, in California, at the Travis Air Force Base, where we were two to a room. When the Red Cross came to each bedside with a portable telephone for us to make calls home to our families, I called my parents to let them know I was okay and was headed home. I wasn't sure when I would arrive or where, but I would try to call whenever I could. My roommate was a black marine in a full body cast. He had a head wound and couldn't speak. It was horrible He had access holes cut into his cast so they could dress his wounds. It was awful. I would never see him again.

After about one day there, all the returning marines and soldiers were on a plane that was full. Our trip began on a DC-6 prop job airplane ride across the country, to my final destination of Hanscom Air Force Base in Bedford, Massachusetts. During this trip, I was placed in my stretcher on the floor of the plane, on the wing. Looking out the window I saw what was to me a helicopter mechanic fixing a huge oil leak. I asked the flight nurse to get the flight engineer, and she did. I informed him of what I thought and said, "That looks like a ten-ragger" (mechanic's term for a "big leak"). He said it was nothing and not to worry. Along the way, we made yet another stop at the army base at Fort Dix, New Jersey. At this stop, I was placed in yet another army medical facility. I thought, *Here we go again.* This time, I was placed on a prison ward—yes, that's right, a prison ward—all part of my "Welcome Home." Picture this returning Vietnam combat marine housed on a prison ward. What's wrong with this picture? I was so pissed off. It was unbelievable. Add to this again my excruciating pain.

Again, we had no nurse for the ward at night but rather one nurse for multiple wards to care for, not only the prisoners but also those of us returning from Vietnam in various stages of medical need. I don't know where the other marines were housed, but I did have a roommate who was handcuffed to his hospital bed, a prisoner we never talked to. However, when he needed to go to the head (bathroom), he called the medic verbally, who eventually un-cuffed him, cuffed his hands together, led him to the head, and then handcuffed him to the bar in the stall to do his business. When I had to go, I was given a urinal and a bedpan. I was appalled at the fact that they even considered putting me in this building. I spent all night asking for medication every time I saw the medic, to no avail, until morning arrived, when they transferred me to a gurney for transport to the flight deck and the plane ride to Massachusetts.

After I was placed on the gurney for my trip to the tarmac, I insisted I would not leave the room until I was given medication immediately. The nurse, then and only then, pulled a syringe from her pocket and injected me. I was pissed that she stood there while I made a scene, insisting on the medication that I truly needed. Thinking back, boy, I sure put up with a lot of shit. And we wonder why guys today suffer from post-traumatic stress disorder (PTSD). The combat experience was bad enough without all this bullshit. Then when they brought us out from the prison hospital, I noticed that we were getting on a different aircraft than the one we arrived on, which was adjacent to our plane. The plane we landed in was having the right engine pulled. Obviously, it was not a normal leak. Damn, I was very angry again!

Chapter 13

Chelsea Naval and VAH Providence

The rest of the trip to Massachusetts was relatively uneventful. We landed at Hanscom Air Force Base in Bedford, Massachusetts, where I was met by an ambulance and taken down Route 128 to the Chelsea Naval Hospital in Chelsea, Massachusetts. I arrived sometime around November 6, 1966, and was taken to the Orthopedic Ward. I was immediately asked by one of the Corpsmen if I needed anything. I asked him to call my parents, which he did, and they were there the next day to visit, along with my girlfriend. I must have looked horrible. During my stay at the Chelsea Naval Hospital, five more nerve blocks were attempted with no results except the residual blindness.

Then after the fifth nerve-block attempt, I said enough was enough. No more. They always attempted to do these nerve blocks on Fridays, painting that awful betadine solution all over my neck and the back of my head, letting me go home for the weekend looking like an ass. Again, I was very embarrassed when I got home with no useful right arm, in extreme pain, and looking like I did. No wonder I didn't want to be seen in public. I had no liberty while in Boston. I had few visitors. My then girlfriend was not allowed by her parents to drive to Chelsea, and both my parents worked, so it was a very lonely and painful period for me.

Initially my trips home were provided by my Uncle Donald Gaudette, who was a state representative at the time. He would have me picked up and taken to the Massachusetts State House, where he would have me introduced to the House of Representatives. When we attempted to enter the first time, the guard would not let me enter, as I did not have a suit coat. That was a rule of the House. My uncle, who was very upset at this rule for his guest, approached the then Speaker of the House of Representatives, and I was allowed in. I sat next to the Speaker's desk and was eventually introduced to the entire House. He took me home a few times. I will always remain great full to my uncle for his dedication to me and for the many veteran-based laws that he sponsored and cosponsored during his tenure.

During my stay at Chelsea, I remember my bed being next to a civilian, Jim, who worked for Springfield Arms. He was in a traction bed, being rotated every hour, as he had broken his back. I remember Jim's girlfriend. She would come almost daily and would bring in fresh fruit for us on every visit. Eventually, she did the same for all the men on the ward. She was the greatest. The naval officer in charge of the hospital at the time wanted Jim to be discharged to a private hospital. As Jim was not a veteran, he did not want to leave. I later found out that Jim's mother was politically connected; she contacted Senator Ted Kennedy's office, who in turn contacted the officer in charge. Jim was subsequently moved to a private room, where they hospitalized officers. Later, when Jim was able to walk again, he visited me and said that he and his girlfriend were to be married in the hospital chapel. I thought that was great.

Newspaper article on my return home

I would now be able to attend my sister's Thanksgiving Day wedding as well as attend the New Bedford High School homecoming football game, held at our rival school, Durfee High School, in Fall River, Massachusetts, to watch my younger cousin play football for the New Bedford High School Whalers. I think we won, but I'm not sure. I was a bit under the weather. I don't remember much about the wedding either, because I was not feeling real great. The pain was awful. It was something I hoped would stop, but I was still disappointed that I felt as bad as I did.

I remember being at the wedding, at least in the church, which was very painful, as I still had my right arm in a cast and was on very limited pain medication.

Picture of me at my sister's wedding

After the Mass, my uncle drove me to Fall River to watch the football game. I remember being on the field watching, again in pain. I remember feeling distant from everyone there—the fans, my uncles. I felt as though I were all alone. I don't remember anyone speaking to me. That day was just a blur. As the game was getting near the end, my uncles took me to my sister's reception, at which I tried to have a drink of liquor, but I couldn't do it. I felt like shit. I don't remember much of the day at all.

During my stay at Chelsea, I was visited by my Marine Corps recruiter Sergeant Robinson. A huge man, he sat on my bed, and we talked for a while. I liked and respected him and had no ill will toward him but rather looked at him with great pride. He said he couldn't continue to see his recruits sent to Vietnam and die or come home like me. He too sat and cried with me. He eventually volunteered for Vietnam and was killed by the Viet Cong.

Newspaper article of Sergeant Robinson's death

Eventually, I was allowed to go home on weekends. I was soon contacted at the hospital by another Marine, George Haymaker, from my hometown, who was also a patient at Chelsea. He was on another ward. His mother had read a newspaper article written about me on November 24, 1966. We got together and made arrangements for his mother to pick us up on Fridays; my father would bring us back to the hospital on Sundays. We did this until I was transferred to the VA in Rhode Island later that year. We never really contacted each other after this and began our separate lives as civilians. It wasn't until sometime in 1975 or 1976 that we would meet up again. George would turn out to be the same marine on the *Iwo Jima* sick bay with me.

After the medical team at Chelsea Naval gave up on the nerve blocks, they decided to unload me onto the Veterans Administration Hospital, so I was eventually discharged from the naval hospital and transferred on orders by the United States Marine Corps to the VA Hospital in Providence, Rhode Island. I was given orders to report to that facility in early December 1966.

Initially, my stay at the VA Hospital in Providence was awful. They decided that what I needed was physical therapy for my right arm, and because I was still an active-duty marine, there on official orders, I had to stay and was not allowed to go home at all, unless approved by the Marine Corps Reserve Unit in Providence, Rhode Island. It wasn't until Christmas that the Marine Corps let me go home for the holidays.

My stay at the Providence VA Hospital was not without incident. I underwent undergoing PT (physical therapy), which included hydrotherapy three times a week. The therapy was worse than the everyday pain that I had. Before I left Chelsea Naval Hospital, I had stopped the pain medication I was prescribed, as I was afraid of becoming addicted. I chose instead to endure the pain. I was taking aspirin with some other medication but no narcotic drugs.

When my PT each day would begin, I would turn my face away from the therapist. I did this for a number of reasons. First, I had no feeling in my right arm except for the pain in all of the joints my shoulder, elbow, and my hand. So I thought that if I looked away, maybe the therapy wouldn't hurt. The other reason was it hurt me even worse, so I cried. Yes, the pain was unbelievable, but I wanted this to work so bad. I wanted the use of my right arm back and would have done anything to get back to what I once was.

Then, one day, during a therapy session, the therapist looked over at me and saw that I was crying. She asked, "Am I hurting you, Dan?"

I didn't have to say a word. She began to cry as well and said she would no longer treat me, as she felt that it was fruitless to continue. The physiatrist agreed, and we began the hydrotherapy treatments.

One morning, I was sitting next to the hydro tank, waiting for it to fill, when the therapist was called away for a telephone call. While I was waiting, the tub filled, so I placed my right arm into the tank, the therapist returned and got very upset with me because the temperature in the tank was too hot, and because I had no feelings in the arm, I hadn't noticed until she removed my arm from the tank. It looked like a red lobster.

While I was hospitalized in Providence, my records were sent to the VA Hospital in Chicago, Illinois (Hines VA Hospital). Here, I'd be assessed for a powered orthotic device to move my arm and hand by external power, a battery. I was rejected by this program because of my residual pain.

Chapter 14

Discharge from the Marine Corps

In January 1967, one of my recruiters from New Bedford, Sergeant Cooper, drove me to the I & I Staff, Third Battalion, Ninth Marines, USMC Reserve Unit, 105 mm Howitzer Battery in Providence, Rhode Island, for my discharge.

The trip there was exciting as we drove there in a full-blown snowstorm. I thought I was surely going to die, but we made it. The Marine Captain who was there to process me discovered while looking through my official personnel record that I had turned down a promotion to Corporal (E-4). He asked why I had done this, noting that all my promotions to PFC and Lance Corporal were meritorious, as was the promotion to Corporal.

I explained to the Captain that while hospitalized at Chelsea Naval Hospital, the Gunnery Sergeant from the Marine barracks at the Boston Naval Yard came to me, stating that I was to receive the promotion and asked if he could keep the stripe for a Marine who would be staying in the Marine Corps. It would be no good to me, he said. Knowing nothing about how this might affect my future, I had agreed. The Captain proceeded to explain to me that because I was about to be medically retired from the Marine Corps' rank, this would determine the amount of retirement pay I was about to receive. *Damn*, I thought, *screwed again, now by the Marine Corps*. The Captain, at that point, delayed my retirement so he could look further into the matter, so we left.

A few weeks later, I was contacted again by Sergeant Cooper to go with him again to Rhode Island. This time, I received my promotion to Corporal E-4 and was "medically retired" as a chapter 61 retiree from the United States Marine Corps, with full retirement benefits. Not a lot of fanfare. I think there were four Marines there. They shook my hand, and that was it. As a result, I was to receive $156 a month from the Marine Corps, which represented 75 percent of my base pay as an E-4 with less than two years' active military service. You see, on discharge, I had one year, eleven months, and six days of active duty. My one month and three days of delayed entry did not count, as I was originally told it would; instead, it was counted as reserve time, not creditable toward active duty.

While at the VA in Providence, I was also able to visit the VA Regional Office (VARO) in Providence to open my claim for service-connected disability benefits. I was a military retiree and was receiving $156 per month, or 75 percent of my military base pay from the Marine Corps. I was instructed to contact the VA for compensation. At this point, *no one* had contacted me about assistance with this claim, not at Chelsea or Providence, so I went to the VARO on my own to apply. This too was a bad experience. While I waited with all the other veterans to be seen by a VSO (veteran service officer), my pain again was awful. Remember, I still had my right arm. When I was finally able to see a VSO, a female, nonveteran, she said she was sorry, but the VARO could not help me because I had not yet been rated by the VAMC for loss of use or any other disability.

Needless to say, like most returning veterans, I didn't know the VA system and was not instructed as to where to turn. I was extremely upset that she was turning me away like that. I must say, I was not very nice to this lady. I yelled at her, saying, "What do you people want me to do, cut my arm off for benefits?"

She apologized and sought out her supervisor to assist me. He did help me file the application for benefits, which began the process. As I was leaving the office, I did notice that the lady I first spoke to was crying. When I left, I felt bad for yelling at her. This wasn't her fault. I was not rated by the VA until sometime later in June of 1967, after my amputation was completed by the VA hospital in Boston, at the end of May 1967, around Memorial Day.

Chapter 15

Amputation

The next referral by the VA system was from the VA Hospital in Providence, Rhode Island, to the VA Hospital in Boston, Massachusetts, for an assessment by their Amputee Clinic Team. So I was transferred to the VA Hospital in Jamaica Plain, in Boston, sometime in April 1967. During this stay, I was poked and prodded by any number of surgical residents. I did meet marine amputees from my hometown area who were going through what I would soon experience myself.

As a Marine, I had been trained to follow orders, which I did without question. These doctors were trying to help, I thought, so I decided to put up with what they were doing to me, until one day, when I'd had enough. I got up the courage to speak out. Today I tell those who ask that the reason I spoke out was that the resident was a young female orthopedic resident. Their routine was the same on every visit. They would first introduce themselves, sit on my hospital bed to my right, pull a long pin from under the lapel of their hospital smock, and then begin to stick my right arm. With this resident, I finally spoke out. I said I would not look while she stuck me and asked that she please stick me as hard as she wanted, but please don't stick me with the pin in the elbow or anywhere below my right wrist. She said she would oblige.

I turned away from her while she began her examination. A few minutes into the exam, I felt her turn my arm. I begged her again not to stick me with the pin on the hand. She agreed and then proceeded instead to lay the pin on my palm. While looking away I flinched from the pain, so she stopped. When she was done, I looked at my arm to find that I was bleeding everywhere. She helped to clean me up and said she was recommending to the Amputee Clinic that they amputate. The clinic would decide at what level and when this would occur.

I was seen in May of 1967 by the members of the Boston VA's Amputee Clinic Team. This was an overwhelming experience for me, as there must have been fifty people in attendance in the room, none of whom I knew. There were at least thirty nursing students as well as medical students observing, along with ten private prosthetists consulting with the team. There were also the VA prosthetists, the chief of Orthopedic Surgery, the Chief of Rehabilitation Medicine, the Chief of Physical Therapy, as well as other Nurses and Doctors. It was an awful experience for me, half-naked in front of all these people. I had just turned twenty-one that April.

To this day, I remember the two lead physicians in attendance as they were wonderful to me, even at this clinic. They put me at ease even with the devastating news that they had decided to amputate me at the shoulder, ultimately making me a right-shoulder disarticulated amputee. Their theory was that by amputating there, the pain would stop without the amputation. The second alternative was to perform a laminectomy—that is a surgical procedure where they go into your spinal column to severe the nerve that sends the pain signal from your arm to your brain. This would leave me with a flailing arm for the rest of my life, without any feeling.

My thought was I didn't want them cutting into my spinal column, and at twenty-one years of age, I didn't want to carry a useless right arm around for the rest of my life. I thought if I ever fell and broke my right arm, I wouldn't know it until it got gangrenous. This was not an option, so I agreed to the amputation.

The amputation was scheduled for that Memorial Day weekend, Tuesday, May 30, 1967. Memorial Day was officially signed into law by President Johnson. I remember my parents and all my aunts and uncles coming to the hospital a few days before to donate blood. I remember questioning why they were there. They said because they were told by the VA that the VA would not operate until the blood donation was made. This again upset me very much. However, they wanted to help, and I thanked my family for their support.

I awoke postoperatively and asked the attending nurse, "Did they do it?"

I could still feel the pain in my arm, and my left arm was tied down to an IV board, so I couldn't feel around. All I could see was a pile of bandages on my shoulder.

She looked down at me and said, "Yes, it's gone."

I thought, *Then why can I still feel the pain in my arm?* The nurse gave me sedation, and I dozed off. When I woke up a few hours later, I couldn't feel my hand, and as time went on, within a few hours, I lost all feeling in my arm. I was pain-free for the first time in over nine months.

Just before my surgery, I was contacted by one of my uncles, who had been contacted by a local New Bedford Veterans organization. After the Memorial Day parade, they wanted a Vietnam veteran to read the names of the eight men from New Bedford who had been killed in Vietnam up to that date. They were told that I would not be available because of the pending arm amputation. I knew I couldn't do it anyway. This is because I knew two of the men who had been killed in Vietnam: Robert Gonneville, USMC on Panel 29E, Line 58, and Norman Beaulieu, USMC on Panel 21E Line 31, both killed in 1967.

I was discharged three days after my surgery without any problems and went home for the first time pain-free. It was great. Now, I'd need to learn to live my life as a lefty, having been right-handed. This, too, was initially devastating. I couldn't do a damn thing with my left arm— write, throw a ball, tie my shoes, dress, tie a tie, eat. I had to learn everything all over again.

After amputation, I was reassigned, to the VA Hospital for Occupational Therapy. I thought the Occupational Therapist at the Providence VA who was assigned to me was going to show me how to do these things one-handed. Instead, she wanted me to use Velcro closures, the newest thing out there, for my shoes, and she told me to buy clip-on ties. I thought she was old-school.

This isn't what I expected. I thought they were going to teach me how to do these things with my left hand. So now I found myself in the position where I need to teach myself these things, because they either didn't know how to do so or didn't want to waste their time teaching me. I began this process on my own, learning how to dress, tie my own regular tie, eat left-handed, and tie my own shoes with one hand. I was never offered any social work, nor any psychological or psychiatric intervention, nothing! Just go home and live your life—no VA contact person for compensation benefits and nothing by either VA hospital.

Years later, while I was working at the VA in Providence, Rhode Island, I was contacted by the local VA librarian, who was getting rid of some old books. She asked if I was interested in any of them. I said sure and discovered that one of those books was titled *The One Hander's Book*, purchased by the VA in 1970, just a little too late for me. Maybe they bought it because of me—I don't know—but it describes techniques for all the things I wanted to do and eventually taught myself to do.

After my amputation, I returned to the VA Regional Office in Providence with my arm now amputated. I saw the same female VSO. I asked her, "Now what do I have to do?" and I apologized for my previous visit. I had my compensation exam done at the VA in Providence soon after this visit. Again, I was never contacted or recommended by any veterans' organization, or anyone from the VA, for that matter, before my own visit to the VARO. I had my claim adjudicated and was given a 90 percent combined disability rating with loss of use of my right arm (minor) at the shoulder, in addition to other disabilities. This was finally done in 1967.

I was just glad that it seemed this was now over and I could begin my life without the pain I had for over nine months. I would discover years later that the VA had made numerous errors when adjudicating my claim. The word *minor* always bothered me. How can the VA consider the loss of one's right arm for a right-handed person a *minor* amputation?

Without guidance from others who understood compensation, I had nowhere to turn. Then, in December 1967, I was issued my first artificial limb by the Boston VA Hospital. Again, this without any instruction from anyone in the VA Hospital system, just my seventy-something-year-old Prosthetist, who worked with me diligently to develop the skills I'd need to function with my new arm. He was great. I will always remember Mr. Sam Polsky, my first prosthetist. Because of my own personal frustration and embarrassment, I never wore that limb with any regularity for about a year. My expectations were higher than my prosthetic limb was capable of performing, and the effort to work the limb was, at first, very difficult.

Chapter 16

Postal Employment

Now I'm home and need to do something with my life. What, I don't know, so in early 1968, I took the written postal exam at the New Bedford Post Office. I received a score of 98.6. I thought that my score was very good, especially since I had problems still with concentration. I was eventually offered a job in the New Bedford Post Office, my home town. I thought, shit, this would be great, so I reported for work there. They took one look at me with my one arm and said, "We don't hire handicapped people." I was shocked and very pissed off. Remember, this was before equal employment opportunity. I was a disabled Veteran.

I married my first wife in July of 1968, and because of this, we made plans to move to California soon after the wedding. Her family was not happy with that decision. I then had my score transferred to the Long Beach, California Post Office, where we were planning to move in August of 1968. I was using a friend's address in Long Beach for mail.

Upon arrival in California, after driving across the country, which took us a week, we found a small one-bedroom apartment in Long Beach. My wife found employment, and I had a letter waiting for me telling me to report for a clerical position at the Long Beach Post Office. I reported to the storefront office downtown, where the interviews were to be held. The human resources person said while speaking to the potential employees, "Everything in the post office is set up for right-handed people, so if you're not right-handed, you are going to have to learn to be."

I raised my left hand, and the gentleman proceeded to come back to me and asked me, seeing no right arm, "Is that service connected?"

I said "Yes, Vietnam,"

He then said, "Wait until we're done with the rest of the interviews, and we'll interview you last."

I thought, *Oh shit, this isn't going be good, and it wasn't.* They said the same thing I had heard before: "We've hired disabled people in the past, and it didn't work out."

I pleaded with them, and then I said, "I fought in Vietnam only to come home and be denied employment." I then said some not-so-nice things to the four folks sitting there, threw my paperwork on the table, and left.

I needed to work for rent money, so I went to the McDonnell Douglas aircraft factory in Long Beach. A friend took me there. I thought with my background as a marine helicopter mechanic, maybe I could get a quality-control inspection job in the factory. The HR application building was in the middle of their giant parking lot. I was given an application, which I filled out and presented to the HR person, who proceeded to tear it up and throw it in the trash in front of me.

"We don't hire crippled people," he said.

My friend had to pull me off the counter and away from the asshole.

During this time, my wife had found employment almost immediately as a secretary.

A few days went by. Then, the Thursday following my brief interview at the post office, I received a telephone call from the Long Beach Post Office HR chief, who asked me if I had a valid driver's license. I said, "Yes, and I have driven across the country." He said that they had a job for me as a special delivery messenger and I needed a valid driver's license. I told him, "I can start tomorrow."

He said, "You can come in tomorrow to fill out paperwork, but you would start on the following Monday."

When I reported the next week for work, I soon discovered that I would be working with two other men from 4:00 p.m. to midnight. One of them had lost the use of his left arm and kept his flaccid hand in his pocket. This was a congenital disability; he was not a veteran. He was born like that. The other guy was a World War II veteran who'd had three of his fingers shot off during the war. Both men were on the

Safe Driving Committee in the Post Office and had been for years. I was in awe.

As the new guy, I took all of the deliveries that no one wanted to do, such as "dog letters." These were letters delivered to folks with dogs who attacked their postal carriers. Until the dog was leashed, they would have to get their mail at General Delivery at the Post Office downtown. These envelopes were stamped "DOG." It always amazed me that we had to deliver these notices in the evening, not knowing anything about the animal except he had attacked the regular daily carrier. We also delivered past-due letters to folks who owed money to companies like Sears. None of these folks were thrilled to see me. Add to this evening delivery, and I was very nervous.

After a year there, my wife became homesick. Also, we wanted to start a family and wanted to have them back home, so I applied for a transfer to the New Bedford Post Office back in Massachusetts. They eventually called me and asked if I could sort mail as a clerk. I said, "Yes, of course," but I didn't have a clue how I was going to do this. During my time in Long Beach, I began wearing my artificial limb and was getting more and more comfortable wearing it.

I was eventually approved for the transfer back to Massachusetts; however, when the Long Beach HR folks got the news, they came to me and asked me to stay on there as a clerk. I said, "No, thank you," as we wanted to go home. Then, in the fall of 1969, I was transferred to the New Bedford Office as a clerk, again driving back across the country. What a transition from carrier to the clerk. I had to learn how to hold the mail with my artificial limb in my hook and use my left hand to sort. I quickly developed a technique that worked for me and satisfied the post office. I did this job for three years, until 1972. To sort mail, I had to modify my artificial limb harness. I tightened it like a cinch on a horse saddle, so every breath I took, my hook would open slightly, allowing me to remove a letter and sort the mail at the rate the post office required.

One of the worst things for me in the post office as an amputee was studying for my two scheme exams. As I was married and we had our first child, a boy, Christopher, who was born in March 1970, I needed to study every night. My livelihood and my family depended on it. Management was not happy hiring me. To begin with, as I found out later, my uncle Donald Gaudette, the State Representative, had intervened on my behalf to expedite the transfer, as they did not want to hire me. As a result, being the lowest-ranking employee in the union, they gave me *all* the crap jobs most of the other clerks hated to do. These included unloading tractor-trailers. One day, while unloading one of these trailers full of Sears circulars, which was for the entire city of 90,000 residents, a very large and heavy load, I stopped everyone who was with me and said to the other three employees, "Am I crazy, or is it strange that the only female in the office, the only above-knee amputee, and the only below-knee amputee—both with over twenty years of service—and myself are the only ones here unloading this truck?"

Both amputees also were veterans, one a combat amputee who was a navy veteran who lost his leg in the Pacific because of a Japanese kamikaze. The other lost his leg in an army training accident. I said to them that while we were out here, there were others in the office sorting mail with much less seniority than the two amputees and the woman— and why were we working to unload these heavy bags? We did unload the trailer in record time, which pissed off management. Discrimination was not given a thought by the post office back in those years.

My first attempt at the scheme test did not go well at all for me. I was extremely nervous when I went in on that day. I had asked the floor boss to go to the superintendent of mails to take the test as required. He then okayed it, so I went into the superintendent's office. He asked me what scheme I was there to take. I told him the city. He took out the cards for the test, then sat at his desk behind me and started his stopwatch as I started sorting. The test has one hundred cards that need to be sorted with no more than six errors, sorting all within, I think, five minutes. I started the test. I put the cards in my hook and picked up too many, and as I started the test, I dropped all the cards. That was the end of the test. I failed. I was mad at myself, so two weeks later, I went back in again, having learned from my mistake. I retook the exam and passed.

I took my two scheme exams and passed them both, which again did not make management very happy. They were hoping I would fail, which would have given them the right to terminate me, but I eventually passed both with flying colors. I stayed in that position for two more years.

Chapter 17

VA and VSO Employment

During a visit in 1972 to the Providence VA Medical Center's Prosthetic Service for approval to repair my artificial limb, I was told about a program in the VA system called the "amputee" program. In reality, it was the Prosthetic Management Trainee Program. I knew I couldn't continue in the post office sorting mail; with my rib and lung condition, it was affecting my health. I was told by the Chief of Prosthetics at the time how to apply and that he would send a letter of recommendation to Washington, D.C., on my behalf. I then applied and was eventually accepted into the program as a trainee in 1972, in Boston, working at the VA Outpatient Clinic and the Boston VA Hospital, the same place that had amputated me five years earlier.

My mentor was a wonderful man whose friendship I would cherish for many years later, until his death in 2011. I remember asking him the day he hired me if he was contacted by anyone politically on my behalf. He said, "No, why?" I told him about my uncle. He said if that had happened, he probably would not have hired me. I was grateful for his comments. His guidance and training over the next two years paved the way for me to have a wonderful career working over the years at thirteen different VA Medical Centers all over the country, from Massachusetts to California and back again, as well as a stint in VA Central Office in Washington, D.C., in the Prosthetic Service. Eventually, I retired as the first VISN #1 Prosthetic Program Manager in New England, retiring from the VA in 2002 with a thirty-two-year career, including my two years of military service.

During those training years, my mentor made me aware of many VA Regulations, including, what the term *minor amputation* meant, which was stated on my original VA rating decision. Because of this, along with other mistakes made during my original adjudication, I could now appeal my own claim and receive a status change from *minor* to *major* for my amputation. Other errors were corrected during this same appeal. It was discovered that the VA had *not* rated me for the loss of my right lung. All this had now given me enough total disability to have a combined rating of 100 percent permanent and total disability.

The term *minor* was used because when I had my first compensation exam back in 1967, the doctor doing the compensation exam asked me if I was right-handed or left-handed. I thought at the time that was a stupid question, as I now only had one arm, my left, so I said "left-handed." The question should have been, "Before your amputation, was you left-handed or right-handed?" As a right-handed person, that meant it was my "dominant" limb, which, according to the VA Rating Schedule, made it a *major* amputation, rated higher by that VA rating schedule.

I also learned during my training year that I would be coordinating the newly established Automobile Adaptive Equipment Program. I remember after my amputation being told by the VSO (veteran service officer) at the VA Regional Office that I was entitled to the $1,600 onetime Automobile grant toward the purchase of an automobile, but I was told it "had to be used within the next four years." So, in 1968, I used the grant to buy a new car. Then, in 1972, during my training, I found out that there was no time limit on the grant oday, in 2017, that grant is now valued at well over $20,000.

It was for these reasons and many others that I wanted to work within the VA system, so as to not mislead veterans with those benefits that I was so ignorant about. I'd had no one who I could go to advise me regarding some of these benefits. This is one of the many reasons I have fought for veterans' rights; I've given accurate information to veterans over the last forty-five years. I have worked in the veteran area to ensure veterans, their widows, and their families receive all the benefits to which they are entitled.

After completing my training, my first transfer made me the assistant chief of prosthetics at the VAH Boston, until a position in Providence became available in 1973. I was then transferred to that post as the Chief of Prosthetics. During this time, my wife and I had a second healthy son, in 1974. In late 1981, my divorce was final. Prior to this, our separation occurred at the time of my transfer to California as the Assistant Chief of Prosthetics at the VAH Long Beach. My wife refused to go back to California, and we were not getting along very well. Maybe it was my anxiety and frustration with her or my PTSD—I don't know. I do know we had numerous issues, both personal and financial. I regret to this day leaving my two boys behind, but I tried to remain in their lives, calling them every week and trying to see them as often as was possible, flying home when I was able. Those years were some of the worst times of my life, including Vietnam. Divorce sucks.

In 1980, my wife and I separated, and I filed for divorce. Partially, I believe it was because of my PTSD. It became final in 1981. It was during this time that I met another wonderful lady from Massachusetts. She had made my life better than I deserve. We traveled together again to California for my next position as Assistant Chief of Prosthetics in Long Beach, California in 1981, I was then transferred again. I was to be the next Chief of Prosthetics in, of all places, the VAH, Wilkes-Barre, Pennsylvania. I remember getting a call from the Associate Director in Wilkes-Barre. He asked if we could do a telephone interview, as he had my OPF (official personnel folder) and was impressed by my experience. His only question for me was, "Why the hell do you want to leave Southern California to come to Wilkes-Barre, Pennsylvania?"

I laughed and told him, "We intended to stay there for four to six years, and we wanted to be closer to our families in Massachusetts."

He said, "Okay, when can you get here?"

I told him, "See you in two weeks."

We left California for Pennsylvania, trying to get closer to home so I could see my children more often. It was during the year in Pennsylvania that my wife and I were married.

Leaving California was difficult for both my wife and me, as we had become very close to many employees and friends there, especially my boss, Glenn Burrer. He was like a brother to me and a father to my wife. He and I worked very well together. We were a great team. He was a quadriplegic veteran who worked every day and took very little time off. Knowing I was a former Chief, he gave me a great deal of latitude and responsibility. He had just been promoted to the Chief position and felt I knew more about some of the processes than he did, because his former Chief had not allowed him to do some of the things that an assistant should be responsible for. He and I both learned a lot from each other. He passed away a few years after we left after a fatal fall off of his wheelchair van lift.

After settling in Wilkes-Barre, Pennsylvania, in 1983, we eventually married on July 2,2983 and bought our first home together. Prices there were low compared to California's real estate, where we had rented for the time we lived there. And we expected to be there for the four to six years, we stated. We had to stay at least a year. While we were in Pennsylvania, we would drive home every weekend to see my boys and visit with family. I saw every football game on Friday nights and almost every baseball game. We always stayed with family, both hers and mine.

In 1984, I received a call from the Director of the Prosthetic and Sensory Aids Service, VA Headquarters, in Washington, D.C. He asked if I would be interested in a position in the Prosthetic Service in the position of a Program Analyst. I found out later that my mentor from my Boston days, who had held that same analyst position, had recommended me for the job before he left for retirement. I said that I was very interested in the position, as this was my goal when I had applied for the management trainee position back in 1971, so after thirteen months in Pennsylvania, we found ourselves in Washington, D.C. I enjoyed the Washington position as a Program Analyst. All the moves from California were again our attempt to get closer to our home and family.

During this same time, my wife had also found better and better positions working in the VA system as well as in VA Headquarters. She ended up working for General Counsel, who are the VA Lawyers. After three years in D.C., in 1987, I received a call from the Chief of Prosthetics in Boston, with whom I had originally trained in 1972. Tony G was himself a US Marine, a leg amputee who had lost his leg in Vietnam. He stayed on as the Assistant Chief and eventually became the Chief. He was a very handsome Italian from Somerville, Massachusetts, who was now dealing with cancer, and it had metastasized. He was in a great deal of pain he decided he was going to retire now. He called me in Washington, D.C. to see if I would be interested in his job. I told him not to worry about me, that he needed to focus on himself and his recovery. He said if I was interested, he would tell his Director who we had both worked under in 1972, and let him know that I was interested. I said yes, I would be, so he called his Director, who in turn called my Director. The result was a transfer back to Boston.

My Director in Washington, D.C. was not happy with me leaving. I told him it was a chance to go home, as my wife and I wanted to have children and the home was where we wanted to raise them. He said he understood and agreed to the lateral transfer without advertisement. When we arrived back home, we visited Tong G in Boston and went to breakfast with him. He looked awful. He had lost so much weight that he was wearing his fifteen-year-old son's clothing. It was an awful sight, seeing him like that. My wife cried all the way home. Tony passed away shortly after his retirement, never getting VA approval for the Agent Orange cancer that took his life at such a young age. He was a 0311 grunt in Vietnam. What a great loss.

During my years in Boston, my wife gave birth to our two children, a daughter and a son. They are now both working and have great careers, as do my two older boys. My wife and I now have eight grandchildren, who we are very proud of and love very much.

In Boston, I also met and worked with another grunt Marine Vietnam amputee by the name of Anthony S. He was hired by me as a trainee from the VA Boston Regional Office. During one conversation with him, I found out that he was in the same unit as Norman B. He, in fact, had lost his leg trying to pull Norman out of danger after he was hit, not realizing he was already dead. He is also on the Vietnam Wall, on panel 21E, line 31. Anthony was a great tri-track skier. He and his wife and three children took us with them, skiing to Mount Sunapee, New Hampshire. We made great memories as our two children would learn to downhill ski. I would meet up with Anthony S a few years later.

In March 1989, I made the decision to leave a very good career with the VA. I withdrew my retirement and invested it in a private firm. This lasted about two years and was not a good experience. However, because I did not burn my bridges and left the VA on good terms, I was able to write to the Prosthetics Service in Washington, D.C., to ask for a position, if available, in New England. I knew that for years, the department had been trying to establish a Prosthetic Service at the VA Hospital in West Haven, Connecticut, the only Blind Rehabilitation Center facility on the East Coast. They issued millions of dollars in prosthetic equipment annually, this without any administrative leadership. As a result, with my background and my references from Hospital Directors in New England as well as the Regional and District Directors in New England, I was hired to be the first Chief of Prosthetics at the West Haven, Connecticut, VA Hospital in 1991 to develop that program.

I was then able to buy back my government retirement; however, because of the interest rates in the 1980s, I had to pay back much more than I had originally withdrawn. What a financial mistake that was. I drove every day over 200 miles to Connecticut from my home in Massachusetts. In that time, I missed only a day and a half of work because of automobile breakdowns. The Hospital Director was very pleased with my work ethic until, in 1992, I was asked to take the position at the Brockton/West Roxbury VA Medical Centers as the Assistant Chief, Prosthetic Service. What a change—more money, a higher grade, and a twenty-five-minute drive to work. In 1992, I was working back in Massachusetts.

One of my responsibilities during my tenure at the Brockton/West Roxbury facility was to act as the Administrative Assistant to the Medical Center Director, a position I was asked to hold temporarily. I did not volunteer for this during my tenure. I was then asked to coordinate the Medical Center's first retreat, which comprised both the administrative and clinical Service Chiefs, to be held at a hotel on Cape Cod. This was when I was told about a videotape entitled "Overcoming Adversity" by J. Charles Plumb, a Vietnam veteran and former prisoner of war. It was a moving motivational video regarding veteran service. The Director approved this video, and all the participants watched this as I used it as a forty-five-minute filler. Soon after the retreat ended, every service chief, both administrative and clinical, wanted a copy to show at their individual staff meetings. It was a huge success.

My VA career took me first to Boston, Massachusetts, as a management trainee and as a staff prosthetic manager, VAH Providence, Rhode Island, as a chief, VAH Long Beach, California, as an assistant chief to

VAH Wilkes-Barre, Pennsylvania, as a chief, then to the Washington, D.C., VACO as a program analyst in prosthetics. Then it was back again to VAH Boston as chief, then to the Boston VA Outpatient Clinic, then a brief sabbatical to the private sector. I left there to go back into the VA system at the VAH West Haven, Connecticut, as the chief, then to the VAH Brockton/West Roxbury, Massachusetts, as an assistant chief. Then I was back again to the VAH Providence, Rhode Island, as a Chief.

It was during my second tour of duty at the Providence VA Medical Center that I would meet once again with Navy Corpsman Joseph Magriby. Years earlier, I had attempted to seek out Joe at his home in Fall River, Massachusetts, only to be told by his mother that he had met and married a Canadian nurse and moved to Canada. This was in the 1980s. Now, in 1996, while working in prosthetics, I got a call from Rehabilitation Medicine, as they were in need of a wheelchair for a veteran who was here from Florida and had been diagnosed with lung cancer. I asked the veteran's name and was told, "Joseph Magriby." I was shocked. I asked if he was there now. They said yes, so I said that I would bring the wheelchair to them immediately. When I walked into rehab, I approached Joe and his wife. I said, "I'm sure you don't remember me, but I remember you." I asked the wife whether she was a Canadian nurse. She looked at me and began to cry. I said to Joe, "You were my corpsman on the *Repose* and took great care of me. You mailed my sister's wedding present home to New Bedford for me. I tried to look you up, but you had left the country."

Joe was hospitalized at the VA a few days later. I asked an embroidery friend to make a hat for me with the corpsman caduceus and "Doc Joe" above it on the front of the hat. When I got the hat, I went up to oncology to see Joe. He had lost his hair due to the chemotherapy. I told him this wasn't a big thing for him but it would mean a lot to me if he would accept this hat as a token of my appreciation for what he did for me thirty years earlier. Joe took the hat and thanked me. I left abruptly as I was about to cry. When I got back downstairs to my office, there was a man waiting to see me. It turned out to be Joe's brother. He thanked me for the hat, as Joe too was in tears and very happy to receive the gift.

Joe died shortly after this. I was then visited by his widow and his three adult children. His wife told me that for all the years they lived in Canada, Joe flew the American flag on a pole in front of their home every day, much to the dismay of the neighbors. The family requested to hold a memorial Mass at the VA chapel and asked if I would like to do Joe's eulogy. I was pleased and scared. I said, "I don't know what to say. I knew Joe for thirty days of his life."

Joe's wife said, "Just tell the story of how you met."

So I did Joe's eulogy. Joe died on Veteran's Day 1996, a true American hero.

Little Compton

JOSEPH MAGRIBY, 50, of 6 Ocean Drive, a general contractor, died Monday at home. He was the husband of Suzanne I. (Lapierre) Magriby.

Born in Fall River, Mass., he was the son of Joseph Magriby Sr. of Fall River, and the late Julia (Kogud) Magriby.

Mr. Magriby was raised in the Corky Row section of Fall River. He had resided in Little Compton since June, previously living in Montreal, Quebec, Canada, where he was a general contractor with Cromwell Construction Inc. He was a Navy veteran of the Vietnam War.

Besides his wife and father, he leaves two sons, Eric Mario Magriby and Saleem Robert Magriby, and a daughter, Asia Anne Magriby, all of Little Compton; a brother, Stephen Magriby of Tampa, Fla.; and two sisters, Kathryn Magriby of Fall River and Carolyn Corby of Lenox, Mass.

A memorial Mass will be held on Friday at 11:30 a.m. at the Veterans Administration Medical Center Chapel, Chalkstone Avenue, Providence.

Newspaper obituary for Joe Magriby

At the end of my VA career, I was selected to be the first VISN #1, New England, Prosthetic Program Manager, responsible for a $40 million program at all eight VA facilities in New England. My career might seem confusing, but just know that every move I made was somewhat calculated, providing not only a higher and higher salary but also experiences that cannot be matched in today's VA system.

On September 11, 2001, I decided after the Twin Towers were hit that it was time for me to retire. This occurred while I was on yet another VA travel status in Indianapolis, Indiana, along with more than fifty disabled veterans from all over the country. We were about to begin our first morning session when the hotel staff informed us about what was happening. They also brought a television down to where the meeting room was. We watched in horror as the two planes struck. I immediately called home to tell my wife I was okay and would be getting home as soon as possible. I felt my PTSD heightening. I called the airport only to find out no planes were arriving or leaving *any* airport.

I reached out to a work friend, Chris N, who had not yet arrived. He said no planes were leaving and he would not be coming. I then informed him that I had called every rental car agency in the city, and none would rent a car one way. He then said to me, "Don't you have a class B driver's license?"

I said, "Yes, why?"

He said, "How about a truck?"

I started to call truck rental companies and found a company just outside the city limits. They gave me a military discount for a brand new ten-foot box truck.

So early the next morning we were off to the rental agency. The other guy was from Vermont and needed to get home as well. He flew out of Manchester, New Hampshire, where he had left his car. He wasn't happy riding in the truck, so I said, "Either you come with me or find your own way home." He decided to ride with me.

Then as I pulled up to the Manchester airport entrance, a state trooper was there and was not happy to see us. I got out and told him I was dropping him off for his car and that the only thing in the truck was our two suitcases. The trooper was very cautious. With his hand on his sidearm, he allowed us to open the back to retrieve the suitcase. I immediately left Manchester, only to get a call from my boss at the VAH Bedford, Massachusetts, headquarters for VISN #1. The doctor said she was calling to make sure I was okay. I said yes and I would be stopping by to see her that afternoon. She said that was not necessary, but I said I needed to speak to her.

I informed her that I would be retiring the following year, giving her advanced notice, so in July 2002, I retired from the federal government service as a general schedule (GS-14). My starting salary was as a GS-6 step 6 trainee in 1972. What a great career, with my military time totaling thirty-two years.

Earlier in 2002, I was to discover that my experience with veteran benefits was needed elsewhere. In September 2002, I was hired by the City of New Bedford as their Director of Veterans' Services and Veterans' Agent. I thought this was a good fit, and I soon hit the ground running. During the interview process, I was told by the city council that they felt that the veterans' agent needed to do more outreach. When I started, the office had fifty-three clients receiving benefits from three other office staff. I worked for the city for the next eight years, again retiring on October 10, 2010, leaving the office with more than 530 clients. Our budget went from $160,000 a year to over $3 million, with no added staff. I was very proud of what we had accomplished.

Shortly after this, I was contacted by my Town Selectmen, who asked me if I would be interested in being the town's VSO, as ours was retiring. I accepted this position in 2012, working there until 2015, when once again, I resigned. However, to this day, I continue helping veterans and acting as a mentor for other VSOs in our area. I love doing good things for veterans and hate seeing veterans being treated poorly by those who are paid to treat them and their dependents with dignity and respect.

Chapter 18

Sports and Getting Older

Over the years, I tried to be very active with regards to sports activities, starting back when I returned from Vietnam as a very young amputee. I had the desire to participate in sports, as I said previously. I played softball in a beer league, which developed into one of the biggest and most competitive men's slow-pitch softball leagues in our area. I was the president of the league we were in. Then I met with two other leagues, with the intention to merge all three, which was a huge success. This new league was called the Tri-Town Softball League. We had thirty-six teams from all over the area. I met some great men back then and still have friendships to this day.

I also participated as a team sponsor, manager, coach, and player for many years. Our team won the league championship in 1976 and also won a regional softball tournament, which was very gratifying for all of us. Some of those men have now passed away. Some are still around. Those were some of my greatest memories.

With every work move that I made during my VA career, I sought out a softball team to play on. I remember my first move, to California. I read an ad in the local newspaper seeking teams in the local slow-pitch softball league, so I called the number and asked that if anyone was looking for a player. I was available. A week later, I received a call from a guy who asked me a lot of questions about my softball experience. He seemed impressed. At the end of the conversation, I had to explain to him that I was an arm amputee and if he would allow me to try out. He could just tell me if I wasn't needed, but I wanted him to let me show my skills and abilities first. He agreed to this and told me where and when the next practice would be.

When I showed up at the designated practice field, I knew with my postal experience that this part of Long Beach was in a not-so-good neighborhood. As I parked my car, the field was lit up, as it was late at night. I noticed that the players on the field were *all* African Americans, except for two men. I got out, put on my spikes, grabbed my bat and glove, and introduced myself to the guy, who I thought was the coach. He was one of the two white guys. His friend was the only other white man there except now for me. The looks I got from the rest of the team were a bit funny. I think they had never seen a one-armed man before, let alone one who played softball, and I was white. The coach asked me what position I played. I said first base and catcher. I later found out that his friend was the catcher on the team.

At the tryout, I shagged fly balls with the team, then played some first base. The guy at first when I showed up was a huge African American, who I was told later had a tryout with the Yankees, so I thought my chances of playing first base was slim to none. He was outstanding. Then they asked me to play first base. During ground-ball practice at first base, the coach seemed to be hitting ground balls softly to me, so I yelled to him, "Is that all you've got?" He started hitting harder and harder, and I caught everything he hit. Then they asked him to hit some pitches. I was what I called a punch-and-Judy hitter: I had good bat control back then and could also hit for distance when the outfield cheated in on me. I hit very well that night. I even impressed myself, but I wasn't sure about the rest of the team. When the practice ended, I walked to my car. Nothing was said to me, but I noticed the rest of the team was gathered together talking. As I was taking my spikes off and tying my sneakers, a few of the team with the coach approached me. They stood for a while, watching me tie my shoes with one hand. I think this shocked them. They asked me if I was coming back to the next practice. I asked them if they wanted me to come back. They said yes, so I was introduced to the rest of the team. They were all great guys, and I became a member of the TNT (The Neighborhood Team).

The league we played in was the Long Beach, City Recreational Park League. They had four seasons—winter, spring, summer, and fall, each consisting of twelve to fourteen games. Every team was placed in a separate division—A, B, C, and D. A division was the best, down to D division, for new or poor teams. I was familiar with this, as this is how we ran our league back in Massachusetts. If you won your division, you would go up to the next division; if you were the worst team in your division, you would drop down to the next lowest division. We started in division D. However, we had some really good ballplayer, guys who'd had Major League tryouts, as I had discovered previously.

As time went on during the seasons, we moved up, winning our division. I played as a sub, catching and hitting. I remember having a few plays at the plate, putting guys out and hitting base hits with men on base. The coach's friend was, in my opinion, a lousy catcher, and he couldn't hit worth a damn. I just enjoyed being there and playing when I could just watch the rest of the team play so well. One game, the players approached the coach and told him I should be the starting catcher. If not, they were all quitting the team. Obviously, they saw what I did about the coach's friend. I was shocked that they would do this but pleased. The coach wasn't happy, so I told him I would not be back after that season. I told the players that I appreciated their support but didn't want to create a rift or be a distraction.

Soon after this, I was approached by one of my VA employees, who asked if I wanted to play with him on a team in a different league. Paul H had a sponsor, and they were looking for players. It was at this time that I bumped into a guy I went to high school with, Lionel M. We also played baseball in high school and later softball. He was now living in Long Beach. He was a very good outfielder, so I asked him if he wanted to play softball with us. He was ecstatic at the chance to play again, so we played together and had a great time. During our years in Long Beach, my wife introduced me to the game of racquetball. I soon came to love the sport, and we played every week and sometimes more often. I discovered that this game was easily played with one arm.

Over the years, in Pennsylvania, Washington, D.C., and then Boston, I played both sports. I remember when we left Long Beach. We talked for a bit about how we had lost our arms. He was in a car accident, but before that, he was a racquetball player in college, and he had lost his left arm, but he was right-handed before he lost his left. He was a very good player and kicked my ass, but we had a good time playing the game. After the match, we were in the locker room, showering and getting dressed, when some older gentlemen approached us and asked us if we were twins. He was blond, and I had black hair. We had a good laugh, as this guy was serious.

I joined a league at a very competitive club. There were about eight guys in the league, very small. We had all played each other except for one other guy and me; we were both undefeated and were playing each other for the league championship. I was told by the others that he was not a good guy. He hated to lose and cheated a lot by calling interference when there was none. When the final match started, I looked up in the gallery to see all the other guys from the league there. They cheered every time I scored a point. The match was the better of two to twenty-one and a tiebreaker to eleven, by two points. He won the first game; I won the second. The tiebreaker was tied 10-10 when I scored the last two-point to win 12-10. The guy was so angry he lost that he left the court without shaking hands, which is a tradition. I looked up to the gallery. My wife and everyone up there were cheering. I still cherish that trophy.

We were only in Pennsylvania for the year, as I said before, when we were transferred to Washington, D.C. After we settled into work, we joined the Crystal City Racquetball Club in Virginia. We played racquetball there. What a beautiful club. We also played softball with a VA coed team on the Washington Mall. The club was very nice, comprised mostly of military personnel and civilians. It was hard to tell them apart, although I did stand out a bit because of my amputation. I would be getting dressed in the locker room and would see men watching while I tied my racquetball shoes. I must admit, I enjoyed entertaining them with my ability.

At this facility, they had what was called a "challenge court" one evening a week. This was where you signed up to play and were assigned a court and an opponent. If you won your game, you stayed on the court to play the next challenger. If you lost, you sat out until assigned to another court, so winning kept you playing. I usually faired very well and would play two to three games before I tired and lost. The softball games were fun, mostly entertaining. Afterward, we went out for adult beverages.

At work, I met some very good men. Some I still talk today, especially through social media. We had a lot of fun at work. Don't get me wrong. The work was very challenging and difficult at times. It was exciting and challenging getting to affect the national prosthetic program, very gratifying. And going to the central office in Washington, D.C., with eleven years of experience in the field brought a perspective that many men I worked with did not have. Some didn't even have any field experience in prosthetics. I truly loved the work.

Chapter 19

My Disability Worsens

After all the years of playing softball, downhill skiing, racquetball, and wearing an artificial limb, my left arm, my so-called good arm, began to weaken. I'm not sure when exactly it started, but I do remember in 1996 while playing softball, I missed a pitch and immediately felt excruciating pain in my left shoulder I could barely drive home, as I was by myself. A few days later, I drove to the VA Medical Center in Providence, Rhode Island, where they gave me cortisone shots in the shoulder, which did not help. I later had to beg my primary care doctor at the time for an MRI. They did an X-ray and saw nothing broken. The MRI showed, of course, a rotator cuff tear. I had my first surgery at the VA there in Providence, and it was a horrible experience. The pain after the surgery was more than I had ever experienced in the past.

I remember getting a visit from my boss, the Chief of Staff at the VA in Providence. I told her that I would rather get shot again than have this surgery. She told me that shoulder surgery was the most painful operation to have. I can attest to that. Yes, it truly is the most painful. Months later, after healing and feeling much better, probably six to eight months, I started to play racquetball again, although very carefully. About a year later, one morning, while playing doubles racquetball, I felt a pop again in my left shoulder. When I left the court, I could see that my left bicep muscle had dropped down as well. The pain was awful.

I was able to make it home, and I decided to call the doctor who had previously operated on me and repaired my left knee after a skiing accident in 2000. He worked with a group of specialists with a sports medicine group out of the New England Baptist Hospital. He referred me to his shoulder specialist, who operated on me for the second time on my left shoulder. This was done in March 2005. This operation was again to repair my left rotator cuff for the second time. He also reattached my bicep tendon. The surgery was light years better because the pain was managed in a much better way. I was discharged home the next day.

After months of difficult rehabilitation, I went back to work. However, less than a year later, while walking into my home up the side porch stairs at my home, I missed a step and threw my arm out to catch my balance so I would not fall. I heard that familiar pop in my shoulder. Once again, this pain was horrible, so in January 2006, I had my third shoulder repair.

I had my fourth rotator cuff repair performed in December 2011. This wasn't the end of it. While visiting my veteran service officer friend in New Bedford, Massachusetts, before Christmas 2012, I was assaulted by a former alcoholic client, who sucker-punched me, throwing me to the cement floor and dislocating my left shoulder. Now, once again, not only did my rotator cuff tear, but I dislocated my shoulder joint. I was taken by ambulance to the local St. Luke's Hospital, where after X-rays they attempted to put the shoulder back into the joint. I told them this could not be done because of the anchors in my shoulder from the previous four should operations. After seeing this on the X-ray, they had to call in an orthopedic surgeon. They took me to the operating room, where they put the shoulder back into the socket without a problem. I was, needless to say, a bit sore. The tear was confirmed by an MRI provided by the Providence VAMC.

I paid yet another visit to my favorite shoulder surgeon, who informed me that he would not operate a fifth time on my shoulder for fear of infection. Without my other arm, he was reluctant to operate until such time that the pain was so bad I couldn't stand it any longer, so I began to take a lot of medication to sleep and get me through the day. He also said I might need a complete shoulder replacement when I got older.

I requested a second opinion from the VA about my shoulder at the Orthopedic Department. I was first seen by the senior orthopedic resident, who said that he wanted to speak to his chief of orthopedics about my case. After a second follow-up visit, they informed me that I should go back to my surgeon, as they would not touch me either for a lot of the same reasons. So now, I'm living with chronic, constant pain and limited use of my right arm.

All this has led me to file for an increase in my VA compensation. Many people, including some VA doctors, had said to me, "Why are you filing this claim for an increase. You're already 100 percent. You can't get more than that." Hearing this for the first time from a VA doctor drives me crazy. Your job is to tell the folks on the rating board at the VARO what you find medically from a medical exam, not to decide whether I should get more compensation.

The request for PTSD resulted in a consult to the PTSD clinic at the VA Medical Center. They referred me to an outreach center in Warwick, Rhode Island. I agreed and was referred to a counselor, a retired peacetime marine. At our first meeting, he asked me a lot about myself. I told him I had a written biography and if he wanted to read it, he could save some time. He took my bio, and I left with a follow-up appointment. The next time I saw him, he stated that he was impressed by my experience and background. As the weeks went by, it didn't seem he and I were getting anywhere. Then, one day, during a session, he stated, "You know, not everyone who serves in combat has PTSD."

I was flabbergasted by what he said. I told him, "I spent five months in a combat unit pulling multiple medivacs during the day and at night, with more than seventy combat missions. You don't think this might have adversely affected me. Just because I put it behind me and didn't deal with it forty-five years ago, do you think it isn't there?"

I left that session and didn't keep any of my other scheduled sessions with that counselor. I received a call from the chief of the PTSD Clinic at the VA Medical Center, asking if I was okay. I explained to him what had occurred and I said to him that in my opinion, *anyone* who saw combat action like I did, or worse, has some PTSD.

> week.
>
> The Army considers medevac crews to be among the most prone to post-traumatic stress because they see so much pain and carnage. Their job is dangerous: The medic and crew chief must often walk out to stunned or grieving soldiers over uncleared ground and take quick control. Crew members say it messes with their heads when soldiers are maimed.
>
> "Sometimes we feel guilty. But it's just not your fault," says Staff Sgt. Audrey Ramos, 28, a flight medic with a Shadow Dustoff team. "You have to let it go. If you harbor it, if you carry it with you to the next mission, then you won't be able to give everything you need to give to the next soldier who has a chance to survive."

Article regarding PTSD for aircrewmen doing medivacs

How they deal with it is up to them. With me, it was family and work. Following my retirement, that's when things seemed to fall apart for me. I got very depressed and thought more and more about my experiences in Vietnam. He asked me, if he were to assign me to a doctor (PhD) at the clinic itself, would I go? I agreed. That began the first, I believe, real therapy session I ever was exposed to since 1966, over forty-four years later. This experience helped me to understand myself better. I live life now enjoying what God has given me—family, reasonably good health, and a life of good deeds helping others and loving life itself (see article on PTSD 20).

My goal at that time was to get two things on my record. The first was to get rated for the PTSD that I know I have had for many years, as I was never rated for PTSD. The second was to obtain loss of use for my left arm this as a result of the multiple surgeries, all based on the fact that having lost my right arm at the shoulder, using my left arm for everything I did in my life every day was too much of a burden. I filed this claim with the encouragement of my surgeons, who wrote numerous letters to the VA on my behalf, supporting my claim.

In October 2004, I began my quest by opening a claim for additional compensation against the VA for "loss of use" of my left arm, along with other medical issues that have since developed because of Agent Orange and my combat experience in Vietnam.

I opened this claim with a good friend who worked with the American Legion as a national service officer, who I believe had forgotten more about VA claims than most NSOs could possibly know today. He was a Korean War veteran, was a former United States marine, and was soon to retire. I remember when we were to have our first appeal. After our first of many denials we were to present on a video teleconference at the VA Regional Office in Providence, Rhode Island, with a Board of Veterans Appeals judge in Washington, D.C. Because this was my first time in front of a BVA judge, I asked my NSO what would he be doing. He said to me, "I'll introduce myself and you, and then you can present your case, because you know the law as well as I do." So he did, and I had prepared a written appeal. I thought it went very well, but we were denied yet again. After this, I remember telling my VSO that they wanted me to die first. Well, I'm not quitting this until I run out of appeals or I do die first.

So after many appeals and numerous compensation exams, too many for me to count, we finally received yet another BVA denial, on November 29, 2012. This denial was eventually reviewed without my knowledge by the NVLSP (National Veterans Legal Services Program). They wrote to me saying that if I would agree, they wanted to represent me in yet another appeal. They reported to me that they had found three "clear and unmistakable errors" made by the BVA.

I agreed, and they informed me that the appeal would now go to the United States Court of Appeals for Veterans. If we won our case, the judge could order the VA to pay their legal fees. If we lost, I would pay nothing. On January 15, 2014, a decision was rendered ordering the VA to grant me "loss of use of my left arm retroactive to the year 2011." This after nine years of compensation exams appeals after appeal after appeal, it was finally over. I received my retroactive check in December 2015 after the NVSLP was paid for their time. I remain grateful to this day for their efforts on my behalf.

Unfortunately, this hasn't ended my pain. The left arm is still so painful that I have difficulty dealing with everything. Oh yes, I was also granted service connection for my PTSD. The loss of use also came with the Special Adaptive Housing Grant. I am now considered to be a 100 percent service-connected veteran with an N rating, and there is additional compensation changing my special monthly compensation from the K rating to the N. This results in more compensation for me.

It's not over for me physically, as I have now been diagnosed with osteoarthritis and carpal tunnel syndrome in my remaining left hand, which is very painful as well. It never seems to end. But for all I've been through, I really have no regrets. I am thankful for my career in the Department of Veterans Affairs, serving all over the country, and as a VSO with the State Department of Veterans Services program. In all the cities and towns I've worked, I've been able to help other veterans and their widows. I am very grateful and have great pride when I am approached by folks who remember the help I've given them or their loved ones. Some are friends now. Others are acquaintances. Some are just folks I bump into at the store or on the street. This is why I did what I did. I loved my work and still do. And I have a loving family to support me, including a loving wife. She is my spirit, my life. I love you very much.

I look forward to my Marine Corps reunions, and I enjoy my veteran friends at the Marine Corps League and the Veterans of Foreign Wars, as well as, of course, my helicopter squadron mates of HMM 363. I am involved more with some organizations than others, and that is by choice. I want to continue to give back to my community as well. I hate negative attitudes, although my ability to do hard labor is now limited, I do enjoy fundraising for veteran organizations and charities. Life is still good, and I cherish every day that I was given. Many of the men in this story have now passed on. Those who are still with us I try to keep in touch with thanks to electronic media.

Semper fi.

Credit Thanks to the Local Media Group Inc, d/b/a The Standard Times for allowing the use of the article dated November 24, 1966 special thank to Curt Brown and Lynne M. Sullivan for their assistance

Thanks also to the San Diego Union Tribune Newspaper especially Mr. Jeff Light, Editor for giving permission to use the article in the SD Union newspaper dated April 17, 1966.

CPSIA information can be obtained
at www.ICGtesting.com
Printed in the USA
BVHW030550090720
583298BV00001B/19